RIVER TRIPS, REVELATIONS, AND OLD TREES

Meditations for Men

RIVER TRIPS, REVELATIONS, AND OLD TREES

Meditations for Men

Philip W. Snyder

MOREHOUSE PUBLISHING

Morehouse Publishing
P.O. Box 1321
Harrisburg, PA 17105

Morehouse Publishing is a division of The Morehouse Group.

Printed in the United States of America

Cover design by Laurie Klein Westhafer
Cover image: Glencar Lake Alluded to by W.B. Yeats
        CORBIS/Michael St. Maur Sheil

Library of Congress Cataloging-In-Publication Data

Snyder, Philip W.
        River trips, revelations, and old trees / Philip W. Snyder.
            p.   cm.
        Includes bibliographical references.
        ISBN 0-8192-1827-8 (pbk. : alk. paper)
        1. Christian men—Religious life.   I. Title
BV4528.2 .S59 2000
242'.642—dc21   99-055587

*To my family, who has nourished me
and kept my memories alive*

CONTENTS

Vanishing Places, Living Memories

Some years ago I went up to the attic to scout out some Christmas decorations and discovered a family of mice had made a nest in the midst of the packing. Shades of there being no room at the inn! My boxes in one sense contained dry and dusty memories. But the nest reminded me that memories provide a place for the future to grow and contain a reservoir of strength that gets us beyond the drab in-between times.

Hence it is good from time to time to take down and unwrap our memories. Many of the places and people described are gone or impossible for me to retrace my steps and find again. Nevertheless they continue to germinate new birth. Their seeds of grace are a great gift for which I am profoundly grateful.

Train Watching

I wait for the LORD, my soul waits, and in his word I hope; my soul waits for the LORD more than those who watch for the morning, more than those who watch for the morning.

Psalm 130:5–6

But those who wait for the LORD shall renew their strength, they shall mount up with wings like eagles, they shall run and not be weary, they shall walk and not faint.

Isaiah 40:31

For a real treat on a Sunday afternoon, my father would say, "Let's go and watch for some trains." We would drive to a sandy pull-off, alongside the main line of the New York Central, which stretched from New York to Chicago. We would park the car facing the tracks and listen and wait. Usually, two or three other cars would be there too; undoubtedly, this was a popular family activity.

Trains ran frequently, even on Sundays. We didn't mind waiting ten or even twenty minutes. We knew eventually we would be rewarded. Sometimes it would be a freight train, and the engineer would wave leisurely and smile as he went by. Freight trains of the 1950s carried the cars of dozens of railroads, and we nearly always spotted a car from a railroad we had never seen before or a new paint scheme of a familiar railroad. The cars came in all shapes and sizes, not like the monotonous unit trains of today. If we were really lucky, we might find a car displaying the chalk figures drawn by hobo artists: large figures of cowboys, horses, or even caricatures of the hobos themselves.

We didn't feel the day was complete unless we saw a passenger train go by. A local with a few passenger coaches was okay, but what we really wished for was a name train, like the New England States, or the Wolverine, with baggage cars, stainless steel sleepers, the dining car with passengers looking out at us as they sipped their coffee, more coaches, and last, an observation car with its lighted sign. Usually mingled with the exhaust, cinder dust, and escaping vapors from the steam lines were the smells of dinner from the kitchen

I can't say for sure that Sunday afternoon train watching made me what I am today or profoundly changed my life. Yet, it was not of little value. I learned that waiting, anticipating, and hoping for something could be part of the sweetness of life. An old Chinese saying goes, "Good things come to those who wait." In contrast, patience is not honored in a culture demanding instant gratification. I still have to fight with my own demon of impatience inside me, but the experience of train watching gives me strength to contend, if only I would remember those Sunday afternoons more often.

Trains made me more aware too of a larger world in motion, of others going somewhere on important business. In my bed in the early morning or late at night when I would hear the whistle at that crossing five miles away, I would picture a train rushing past the turnoff, on the way to Chicago or returning to Boston or New York. Even as I woke or slept, the world was on a journey.

Last, and perhaps most important, the trains helped me know that somehow I was connected to that larger world. The tracks were an unbroken band of steel from coast to coast. The wave of the engineer, or the smile of the conductor looking out from the open top half of the car door, affirmed my presence in the world. Someday *I* would be on an important journey. I would sip coffee in the dining car, rushing past others who were waking up, or retiring, or watching by a roadside pull-off.

Jesus began teaching in a small-town synagogue: "The Good News of God is available to you today. The kingdom, the way God intends creation to operate, is working like leaven in your midst. Waiting is not a futile exercise. Hoping is not a delusion. Today, I have been anointed to proclaim release and healing to all, even to children by the side of the road. Today I testify to a new world reality beyond the hills of your birth and culture, beyond even the boundaries of the Roman empire, and you are a part of it."

Most places of worship are small and unpretentious. Yet every Sunday in countless of these places, the good news is announced, possibilities are born, and dreams are ignited. Sometimes revelation means hearing for the first time; sometimes communion is realizing that we have been heard; and sometimes being touched by the spirit involves an awareness that we are part of a body in motion, going beyond our time and horizons.

Trains are not what they were, and there are fewer and fewer dirt pull-offs where you can park by the tracks. They are vanishing places, but still living memories. It's too bad, for I think Jesus would have enjoyed and recommended going train watching on a Sunday afternoon.

Old Trees and Seed

"The kingdom of God is as if someone would scatter seed on the ground, and would sleep and rise night and day, and the seed would sprout and grow, he does not know how. The earth produces of itself, first the stalk, then the head, then the full grain in the head. But when the grain is ripe, at once he goes in with his sickle, because the harvest has come." He also said, "With what can we compare the kingdom of God, or what parable will we use for it? It is like a mustard seed, which, when sown upon the ground, is the smallest of all the seeds on earth; yet when it is sown it grows up and becomes the greatest of all shrubs, and puts forth large branches, so that the birds of the air can make nests in its shade."

Mark 4:26–32

My grandparents lived in an old row house on a street shaded by ancient trees. The trees made an enduring impression on me. Many had partially hollow trunks filled with smooth cement bricks. Some of the trunks were so walled up that the blocks made up over half the tree's trunk. To a child such trees seemed to have an unshakable permanence. In fact, the cement bricks were signs of decay. The tree was dying, and most of the trunk was already dead.

The prophet Ezekiel used tall cedars as an analogy to the empire of Assyria and, indirectly but pointedly, to Egypt too. We have a picture of a grove of trees that are huge but long past their prime. Eventually, they grow so tall that lightning strikes and splits them, the wind blows them over, or they are cut down by invaders for lumber. Like the trees filled with cement, their permanence is a delusion. Only youngsters are fooled.

Jesus' parable of the mysterious growth of seed is an interesting contrast to Ezekiel's analogy of the tall cedars of Lebanon. Jesus offers a picture of a farmer sowing the seed, waiting for it to germinate, going about the everyday chores, eating, sleeping, and watching until the harvest. After gathering the grain and plowing the field under, the farmer is ready to begin over again in the spring.

Jesus loved to compare the relationship between the presence of God and the power of the world with the relationship of seeds and the earth. In part, Jesus wanted to emphasize the incredible generosity of God's grace. God spreads wonderful gifts like the hundreds upon hundreds of seeds that a farmer sows in the field. Jesus also wanted to emphasize the universality of God's love, a love that spreads itself as widely as seeds floating in the air, being carried everywhere by the wind. Yet, just as important, Jesus wanted us to realize that what we see now, what appears to be reality in one moment of time, is emphatically not the whole story. In the winter, the farmer sees frozen ground, and in the spring, acres of mud. But the farmer puts on his boots, goes out, and broadcasts seed upon the field, for he trusts that the fall will bring a sea of golden grain.

The world likes to define things as tightly as possible. It likes to limit and control things. The world likes to define permanence in terms of perennials, like giant trees, attempting to reach the clouds. The world looks no further than the imposing trunk, even if inside the trunk is hollow and most of the wood is dead. It's so easy to be mesmerized by monumental trunks and then be completely devastated when the tree topples. That is why the world always has plenty of reasons to believe things are futile and cannot be any better than they are. The world sees a lot of mud, and wrings its hands.

Most of us from time to time have an uneasy feeling that much of our familiar world may be like a venerable tree patched up with blocks. Many of us have experienced transitions and have seen ancient pillars topple that we assumed would always exist. Plenty of people in today's society feel cheated, jealous, or resentful. We live in an angry age in which many feel that a sacred grove has been cut down. People of faith need to remember that fresh definitions that transcend or go beyond society's assumptions not only have the wonderful potential to free and renew people, they also can threaten people so much as to enrage them.

Jesus suggests that life in the kingdom of God reveals itself like the annuals, the plants that are sown, germinate, grow, and flower from tiny, insignificant specks. It's beyond our imagination how a seed smaller than a fingernail can mature into a sunflower with a giant head of seeds. Beyond logical explanation is goldenrod's habit of always producing a bumper crop, even though no one in the entire country ever plants it or mulches around it. Yet that is how God operates.

Although we prefer to think of ourselves as perennials, we are really annuals. Jesus calls us to pay attention to the seed of our life, to what is deep, to what is not readily apparent. Our hope comes from the seed. God takes mud and makes life. God takes what seems barren and produces a grand harvest. That's what the new life of God's kingdom is like—an abundant kingdom, available like seed slung in every direction from the hand of a sower. In a catastrophic world, when even ancient giants are being cut down, Jesus brings good news, good news to those who are open and receptive.

Thacher Park

It is better to take refuge in the LORD than to put confidence in mortals. It is better to take refuge in the LORD than to put confidence in princes.
Psalm 118:8–9

Each spring, when it comes time to cut the lawn for the first time, my thoughts invariably turn to picnics, hikes, and overnights in the woods. As a child, the approach of Memorial Day not only meant the end of school, it also meant family trips to Thacher Park, a state park in the modest Helderberg hills outside of Albany. For a child, it seemed a timeless place, with the smell of the dried evergreen needles and the faint whiff of creosote from the standard issue wooden picnic tables. As the food was being unpacked and the hot dogs were singed, we would go exploring the trails leading to a small cave and a few modest waterfalls. Later, I would graduate to camping.

I would like to find a movie that shows parents taking their children camping in anticipation of having an enjoyable experience. Unfortunately, most movies of this sort appear to be remakes of *Deliverance*. Amidst startling scenery, innocent campers run into perverts and maniacs, but through feats of stupendous bravery and physical prowess, the campers survive and conquer the dangers, both human and natural, of the river and woods. I suppose we are expected to say at the end, "Wow! What a super guy that Burt Reynolds is," or in the case of *The River Wild* with Meryl Streep, "What a super mom, and dad isn't that bad either!" Yet, why anyone having such a traumatic experience would ever want to return on any river or wilderness vacation, I'll never know. I wonder if such movies aren't backed by developers of large hydroelectric dams. Of course, terrible acts of violence may occur anywhere. Serious crimes in our national parks are increasing. Fortunately, they are still the tragic exception. The woods remain a lot safer than shopping malls, and campers seem to be an unselfish lot.

We live in a society that prefers to separate us into either victims or victimizers, an insidious tendency that promotes an unhealthy self-centeredness. The articulation of one's opinions often becomes more important than a common search for truth. Out in the woods, if the ants get into your potato salad, the mosquitoes threaten to bite off your ear, or the rain gets your sleeping bag wet, it's more difficult to carry on such games. The ants and mosquitoes don't categorize you at all; you are just another link in the food chain. It's not that the wind and rain don't care about the right issues or are not properly sensitized to your history; they just don't know you are there. You may adapt or move to another spot. As long as you don't go home, however, you begin to learn that you will never be the center of the universe. But that's okay, for you can still find satisfaction, pleasure, and contentment.

I don't go on picnics or venture into the woods to make myself uncomfortable. Baked beans mixed with pine needles, and a leaky tent are hardly included in the joys of camping. But often such things lead us to realize that better living is not always a question of chemistry, technology, or self-awareness. Sometimes it's the buzz of mosquitoes and the approach of a thunder shower that lead us to recognize and respect our limits, and to ask ourselves why we are living on earth.

Madison Beach Hotel

Some friends play at friendship but a true friend sticks closer than one's nearest kin.

Proverbs 18:24

I suspect it was a pattern for generations and didn't change until the 1960s. Families would take their week's vacation together, staying at one establishment, year after year. We stayed along the Connecticut seashore at a place protected by the Long Island Sound, a location that offered a gradual soft beach and lake-like waves. The waterfront hotel had a game room with Ping-Pong tables and shuffleboard, and an outdoor clay tennis court. The long, covered front porch filled with rocking chairs was always popular in the evening. Although it was billed as a family resort, many elderly rocked to their hearts' content watching dusk roll over the beach. Bingo night and movie night were popular too.

We had the first floor of a summer cottage. Actually it was the frame of a decent sized house, but it had no finished walls, just the studs, with the pipes and electric wires running through. The furniture was late nineteenth-century cottage oak. Nothing fancy, but very serviceable, no plastic—and today it would make an antique dealer beam. The bathrooms were large and wood-paneled with claw-foot bathtubs, long white porcelain towel racks and toilets that prominently displayed their brand names and models. A damp salt smell hung inside when the windows were closed or when it rained for more than a day. When we walked over to the dining room, we passed the kitchen, which had two large exhaust fans high in the wall. The hot smell of bread and pastry at noon and the aroma of roasting meat at dinner would directly blast us for a moment—a wonderful appetizer.

I would occasionally fish off the stone breakwater and catch small fish called porgies. At least once while we were there, I would give my two or three fish to the cook in the afternoon, and at night the staff would proudly bring them to us under a silver-plated cover and surrounded with lemons and tomatoes carved in the shape of baskets.

It may all sound boring by today's standards, but we didn't think so at the time. The resort was filled with gentle guests and staffed with young college kids. You got to know the wait staff, desk clerks, maids, and other guests. They knew something about your story and you knew about them. There was often something to share from the year before and to catch up on when you returned the next year.

These vacations were not filled with exhilarating thrills, but they were still fun. I can remember only one incident that in some sense might be termed an exciting experience. Friends who came with us one summer loved to eat raw clams. All week long, they tried to persuade me to eat one. To me, clams looked like an awful mess of slime and grit, but finally my friends' persistent assurance that clams tasted better than ice cream wore my defenses down and my curiosity got the better of me. I closed my eyes, took a deep breath, and swallowed one. It did not taste better than ice cream!

I have long since forgiven my friends for such a cruel misrepresentation played on an innocent lad. Yet it was also an introduction to an important lesson. Spiritual maturity involves an understanding that ultimate values do not stand or fall on the opinions of even close friends. We all tend to fear the world's assessment far too much and grant it disproportionate influence in our lives. There have been occasions when I felt pressured to perform because I feared that was what was expected of me, when there was no true outside pressure at all. I had manufactured it all within myself. I wished I had recalled my incident with the raw clam sooner.

The interstate highway system, cheap airfares, and social patterns of work and family all doomed many of those old-time resorts. As people rarely spent more than a weekend in one place, many resorts folded or were gradually changed into condominiums and time-share apartments. The cottages where we stayed are now upscale beach houses with Jacuzzis and air-conditioning. The wood frame hotel was razed and in its place is a snazzy club resort. I could never afford it. The breakwater pier was damaged by a hurricane and had to be demolished. The large rock outcropping where the tide made its mark in the crevices, leaving behind treasurers of crabs, seaweed, and shells in warm pools, and which was our castle, ship, and look-out, is still there.

Something tells me to treasure the experience. You don't remember the good smells from kitchen exhaust fans when you just stay a long weekend at a climate-controlled resort. You don't have friends with you who have the time and patience to convince you to try a raw clam. I rarely see rocking chairs in hotel lobbies, and who builds long outdoor porches anymore? Still, I wonder, if we had more rocking chairs would we use fewer tranquilizers? I am happy that my children have gotten to go to the seashore at some beautiful parks. Yet I worry, have they lingered long enough to notice and remember things that will stay with them decades afterwards? What can they take to put in their permanent memory banks from a three-day weekend on thrill rides at an amusement park, eating dinners out at fast-food places, and spending nights at a chain motel?

Revelation in the Attic

Then I saw a new heaven and a new earth; for the first heaven and the first earth had passed away, and the sea was no more…. And I heard a loud voice from the throne saying, "See, the home of God is among mortals…."
Revelation 21:1, 3

M ost houses built before World War II had large attics with stairs and a regular floor and even a gabled window or two. Attics were used to store all sorts of things of the past—some broken, some just outmoded and obsolete. Items that people didn't know what to do with at the time but didn't want to throw out were also saved for a later day. I think it is a loss if a child does not have a relative with an attic to explore. One of my fond childhood memories is of getting permission from my great-uncle to investigate his attic and of his allowing me to take home all the old *National Geographic* magazines I wanted. Boy, did my parents appreciate that!

As a priest, I have found that the neat thing about living in a church-supplied rectory is discovering what previous incumbents have left behind. Needless to say, I am very wary of people who advertise to clean attics for a seemingly low fee. Rather than being helpful, they often clean out history for a fast buck.

For me, reading the book of Revelation is like going up into an attic and open-ing the drawer of a dark mahogany Victorian dresser that smells of dust and moth balls. The book's language is obsolete and the expressions seem strange. Like exploring a real attic, though, if you keep probing and are willing to put up with the dust and even some mouse droppings, you may rediscover a wonderful trea-sure and wonder why it was ever forgotten. Even what seems at first to be scary can turn out, as we handle it, to be pretty benevolent after all.

Actually, I wonder if the church communities that compiled and preserved the book of Revelation didn't do more than a little attic rummaging them-selves. The people of that time knew that the symbols and language of their larger culture were precipitously losing meaning. They had to go outside their immediate situation and everyday language to find different vessels; they had to search for something that would contain and communicate to others the Good News. So they stretched and shaped the images until they conveyed the hope of the gospel.

These Christians were not nomadic tribes but were established somewhere within the larger Roman empire. They couldn't run away from the threat of per-secution, and they knew of no political force on the horizon that promised deliverance. Yet they took the image of the lamb, an ancient symbol of nomadic life, redefined it to reflect the living Christ, and fashioned a great drama. Bowls, trumpets, and lamp stands were among the props. The elders and creatures made up the choruses.

These Christians in Asia Minor refused to let their own troubled time trivialize their values or make their lives conform to the cynicism of the world. Their world was in dire need and their church in dire straits, but they knew that God had not given up on either one. That's what this drama is all about. Rather than denying history, the early Christians went beyond it and mixed it with hope. Where the waters of history and hope converge, new birth begins. People of faith today may very well have to learn to do as those Christians long ago did. Our world and our church appear in many ways to be under a fierce siege, but God won't give up on either one.

Like an attic, Revelation has plenty of treasurers whose original use we can't explain or understand. That's okay, for although we might not know what all the symbols mean, they may in some way come in very handy to us today, reminding us that life is much deeper than simply what we have in hand.

Unfamiliar artifacts of a century ago keep things in perspective. Yes, we can tell our children, people really did live this way. They devised clever gadgets, and they prospered, laughed, and dreamed dreams, the same as we do. The imagery of Revelation tells us that people under persecution, in a situation without precedent, retained hope. They passed their legacy of keeping faith on to a world they could not imagine even in their most whimsical fancy.

The book of Revelation holds treasures for us to reinterpret, to adapt, to stretch in different directions. Such rediscovery and reuse offer balance, nourish the roots of people of faith, and give us the courage to create new language and journey forward. At the very least, don't deprive your children of the experience of rummaging through a dusty attic. They may look a mess when they are through, and you may find they want stuff you would be embarrassed to put out for a garage sale. Nonetheless, see if you can catch some of the joy in their faces.

The Church Picnic at Six Mile Water Works

When I was a child, I spoke like a child, I thought like a child, I reasoned like a child; when I became an adult, I put an end to childish ways. For now we see in a mirror, dimly, but then we will see face to face. Now I know only in part; then I will know fully, even as I have been fully known.

1 Corinthians 13:11–12

The Six Mile Water Works was a picnic grove and small lake just outside Albany's city limits, surrounded by an area of sandy hills and scrub pine called the pine bush. Hunters would hunt deer there in the fall, and all summer children would roam, building forts, exploring, and playing various versions of cowboys and Indians. In the winter, hermits and rabbits had the place pretty much to themselves, with the exception of weekend skaters who would shovel off part of a pond. It was a frontier, and people respected one another's right to be left alone, neither harassing nor being harassed. On its edge were a Little League ball field, some abandoned farmhouses filled with broken furniture that were used by firefighters to practice search and rescue, and down the road some distance away, the rambling TB sanitarium, a mysterious and off-limits place with a large porch filled with empty rocking chairs overlooking a huge green lawn.

Picnics at Thacher Park were an activity we did as a family, but every June our church would have its picnic at the Six Mile Water Works, and that was a communal obligation. The event was a logistical undertaking approached with the seriousness of moving an army reserve unit to Fort Drum for summer maneuvers. I never realized how important this picnic was to the parish community until I came across old notes and plans of my father, who was for many years the Sunday school superintendent and thereby titular head of the picnic. Since many people did not drive or cared not to drive that far out of town, red-and-cream buses were hired from the Union Traction Company. Lists of food supplies, soda, and paraphernalia for the games were made and checked. Probably 90 percent of the parish participated. It was unashamedly a highlight of the year for both young and old, the only game in town for that Sunday afternoon.

The picnic tables were sheltered under the trees, and a favorite activity while we waited for the burgers and dogs to grill was going through the pine duff and finding bottle caps. Rare and less common soda and beer caps had value and were traded among us. After the food we ran sack races, played softball games, and swam. Some of the more adventurous might take a hike into the pine bush. Toward the end of the day, sunburned and tired, we would pack up and head home, leaving a pile of bottle caps on a table for the next collectors.

I never was conscious that one afternoon would be my last church picnic and that I would never return again. I just waved good-bye, expecting the picnics to continue forever. Yet there was that certain one that was my last.

The Six Mile Water Works is no longer on the frontier. It is still a city park, compressed by highways and wedged among mega-shopping centers on all sides. On the spot where the sanitarium once stood is one of the high-rise dormitories for the state university. One simply can't return. Hermits and explorers have moved on long ago. Of course I moved just as far away. I am now a spouse, a parent, and in various positions of some responsibility. I've experienced varying disappointment and failure as well as the taste of success and triumph.

Significant chapters of our lives often turn without our knowing it at the time. That seems obvious, but it is not so obvious. Perhaps it is just as well that we are not omniscient, or we'd futilely struggle to stay where we are. That is always a grave mistake, the road to spiritual atrophy. I can rejoice in reminiscing because I have moved on. Life is leave-taking, exploring, and finding what comes next. I can smile and imagine that a few of the piles of bottle caps may still be under the pine duff, maybe even in a place a child might rediscover. I know now that communal picnics helped many of us also to collect some neat memories, and when I left for the last time, they were not left behind.

Collecting Peas

For as the rain and the snow come down from heaven, and do not return there until they have watered the earth, making it bring forth and sprout, giving seed to the sower and bread to the eater, so shall my word be that goes out from my mouth; it shall not return to me empty, but it shall accomplish that which I purpose, and succeed in the thing for which I sent it.

Isaiah 55:10–11

Imagine a sower going out to sow. [Some seed] fell on rich soil and produced their crop, some a hundred fold, some sixty, some thirty. Listen, anyone who has ears!

Matthew 13:4, 9
The Jerusalem Bible

In the hot days of July, from the time I was six years of age until I was about ten, I would visit my great aunt, who had a summer home surrounded by the fields of Pennsylvania Amish farmers. Her vegetable garden was her pride and joy, and every morning after breakfast in what became a ritual, we would go out to pick some peas or beans for supper. "Oh, no," my aunt would say, shaking her head, "I don't think there are many peas on the vine today." I would get down on my hands and knees and exclaim, "What do you mean no peas, look at the pods here underneath!" and soon I'd have picked several pint baskets.

Why is a child so good at finding pea pods or wild blueberries? Because a child acts out the point of the parable of the sower. The child expects to find; after all, blueberry bushes *should* have berries, vegetable vines *should* have pods. That's why they exist, to produce fruit. The child isn't jaded by an adult cynical world that complains about an unpromising environment. If a child can easily pick quarts of peas where an adult has rejected the vines as barren, if the most vigorous weeds can grow up time and time again from the cracks in a hot sidewalk, how much more will God, who is a universally generous sower, provide for a harvest? Sure, some seed is going to be devoured or choked off, but there is plenty more, and that will provide a bumper crop of thirty, sixty, or a hundred fold.

Many religious people tend to close off or limit the seats in the kingdom of God. We imply that one has to do this or that, or we draw up what we claim are suitable entry requirements for admission to God's great banquet hall. We expect that God's guest list needs to be thinned. But the lesson of the parable of the sower does a total about-face. It says that God wants us to work in expanding (harvesting if you will) the kingdom of God. God showers the seed in every conceivable place. The seed, like the spirit and redeeming grace of Christ, is for everyone. Then the parable astounds us by inferring that we aren't expected to fertilize or water or protect the seed as much as we are asked to expect to *find* the fruit of God's love in the world around us. It is as if we were invited to an Easter egg hunt. We don't have to provide the eggs, decorate them, or put them around. That is already done. We are in the garden, as it were, to pick the eggs up, to guide others to them, and to share the joy of their discovery and their beauty with one another.

If there were ever a parable for discipleship in a hostile environment, it is this one. The good news is that we don't have to do all the sowing or be responsible for the miracle of new birth and growth of life. That's given. Yes, we are asked to be responsible for the gifts we have received. Yet, we are asked not so much to seek to control the plant that will bear the fruit as to realize and acknowledge its existence. In similar fashion, we are gently invited to experience the healing power of forgiveness, the sense of thankfulness and generosity, the spirit of peace and forbearance, and a whole bounty of wonderful gifts of Christ's grace.

Why *is* Christ discovered in the most unlikely or remote of places? Why do children find the most blueberries or peas? Why does grass grow the best, unfertilized and trampled on, in cracks of sidewalks and driveways? Don't be surprised by any of these things, for they are common occurrences. The answer to all these profound questions is the key to the parable of the sower, and part of the wonderful promise of the commonwealth of God.

Leaf Smoke

In the Lord your labor is not in vain.

1 Corinthians 15:58

I grew up on a residential street with a parkway in the middle. About forty feet wide and running for two blocks, the parkway was an ideal spot for hide and seek as well as kick ball. The street was also blessed with many tall maples of various species, and in the fall, the trees were tapestries of gold, yellow, orange, and red before dumping their colors on our lawns. Fall meant raking leaves. We would rake them into piles and jump into them, raising and tossing the leaves as a geyser sprays water. We would rake the leaves into borders, making houses with rooms, sometimes turning them into mazes. Last, we would rake them into the parkway across from our houses and burn them. A leaf fire has to be constantly fed. You stand by it, and as it burns down, you give it life again. You decide to make it a flamer or a smoker. You can also decide to rake it out and come back to start it another day.

I now live in a newer development where most of the trees are small. What leaves there are, my neighbors blow into piles with large leaf blowers and force them into bags to be taken away or to be transported to someone's compost heap.

In older neighborhoods, city trucks fitted with giant vacuum nozzles suck up the leaves with a mean sound. You can't burn them anymore, anywhere. It is as if we are embarrassed to have them around, much less let our children play with them anymore.

I don't think I learned any profound lesson in simply raking leaves. In the spring there was no sign of your labors. Yet it never seemed to be real drudgery. Though every fall we did it, we felt a little regret when the last of the leaves were burned or an early snow put an end to balmy leaf raking. As children we made leaf raking fun and rarely thought of it as a mindless, routine job, necessary for a healthy lawn. I wonder if leaf blowers haven't changed it into a chore. When I see the rug beaters, chimney brushes, washing paddles, and clothes wringers in antique shops and museums, I think how hard some of the tasks of everyday living must have been for my grandparents. But what we imagine was unmitigated drudgery was not seen by them like that at all. It was just simply something one did.

Perhaps leaf raking is more like life than we'd like to think. There are experiences we have had that our children will not. We all inevitably face repetitive, boring, and inconsequential tasks. Yet how we get through the routine does make a difference. I'm not terribly fond of cleaning pots and pans, but it has to be done, and I've learned not to get resentful or upset when I do them. Some things are a burden only when we make them.

There is a picture in my mind of driving home late one weekend afternoon. People are out in the parkway, tending their leaf fires and the haze of the smoke covers the street. I'd sure like to smell the smoke of leaf fires again. For some people, the smell of incense is a sign of a holy presence, but for me, if I were to die and wake up in a strange place, if I smelled leaf smoke, I'd know I was home.

The Saco River

Therefore every scribe who has been trained for the kingdom of heaven is like the master of a household who brings out of his treasure what is new and what is old.

Matthew 13:52

The Saco River begins in the White Mountains of New Hampshire. Flowing over the boulders in Crawford Notch, it soon changes into a quiet sandy-bottomed river, first through public and private campgrounds on each side of its banks, and then through rolling hills and pasture land. It would not be on any-one's top ten list for the wildest and most challenging ride. But it is perfect for tak-ing young boys and girls on their first canoe trip, and for swimming and camping along its unhurried route. I remember the first canoe trip I was assigned as the trip leader at a summer boys' camp. It was down the Saco to a put-out place called Hiram. I was told we would come to some tall sand dunes a mile or two before Hiram. The campers, I was assured, will love to stop for an hour and run up and down the dunes into the water. The trip itself was uneventful. We camped on a sand bank, taking care to pick one where cows had not been recently grazing. After supper, we hiked back in the woods, found a dirt road, and walked until we saw a farmhouse in the distance. A large red sun hovered above the low hills. We returned, roasted marshmallows, told some ghost stories, and went to sleep. During the night we heard the whistle of a train, telling us that we were not that far from civilization if we had an emergency. I thought of the sand dunes ahead. Would I recognize them? What if we went past them? Just how big were they? What about Hiram, an unknown place by a bridge? What was there? Who lived there? It was fun to dream of it as a place of mystery.

We had no trouble finding the dunes. We drifted around a bend and they appeared, made of fine white-brown sand rising about seventy-five feet. We beached the canoes, and up and down we ran, jumping into the water. From the top we could see bends of the river where we had paddled, winding like a sheepshank knot, as well as look down into the clear water right below. A hundred yards beyond the crest of the embankment were the railroad tracks and highway. As I sat in the shade of a few small trees, my mind took a snapshot that I have never lost.

We had no problem finding Hiram either. It showed the first signs of habitation we had come to since putting in. It seemed to be no more than a dozen or so old houses, a small general store with gas pump, and an ice cream and hot dog stand open for the summer just for campers like us. We hauled our canoes and gear up to a clearing by one side of the bridge and were enjoying ice cream cones when the camp truck came to pick us up.

I don't think of Hiram and the sand dunes of the Saco very often. When I do, it is usually when I am driving home along a rural road from a late evening meeting. There are few cars that pass, and fewer lights from houses. Bounding deer are the real hazard. The young campers I led are now adults, most, no doubt, with demanding jobs and a solid record of accomplishment. Are their lives just too busy for any of them to have made any connections between their adventure on the Saco River and their adventure of transition from youth to middle age? Have any of them reflected whether this summer expedition in childhood helped them as adults to be open and accepting of the twists and turns of reversals as well as to savor the moments of exhilaration? I wonder, when the golden leaves of autumn are gone, the equalizing snow of winter yet to come, and summer seems a long way off, do they ever, like me, think of the sand dunes rising high from the water? When they stay at a motel on a business trip and hear a train whistle somewhere in the distance, do they recall canoeing to Hiram? Despite the cynicism of age, have they retained any keen sense of excitement for the unknown? Through all their travels, have they kept any snapshots in their minds?

Transfiguration: Old Men and Their Straw Hats

Peter said to Jesus, "Master it is wonderful for us to be here." …He did not know what he was saying"

Luke 9:33, The Jerusalem Bible

Years ago, when I visited my grandparents, my grandfather would take me on at least one trip to downtown Lancaster. We boarded the bus a block up from his house and fifteen minutes later got off at the town square. Across the street was the tall bank building. Riding the elevator up to one of the top floors, we walked down a corridor and entered, through a dark varnished door with frosted glass, a room with several rows of wooden arm chairs. My grandfather would take off his summer straw hat and place it on the hat tree, already filled with half a dozen white straw hats. On a shelf across the room, a large oscillating fan gently lifted them with a brief flutter as it turned.

We sat down and looked up to a screen showing a large moving tape, some ten feet long and a foot wide, with many symbols and numbers. Sometimes the tape moved quickly, then it would stop, only to jerk to life again. A sound like a typewriter clattered in sync with the tape's movement. Below the tape was a chalk-board, divided into rows and columns, and usually numbers and letters were chalked on them, too. To me, they were indecipherable and therefore totally unin-teresting. What fascinated me was the machine behind the lighted tape screen and blackboard. One of the men, dressed in white shirt and suspenders, would let me go through a little door by the board, and there ticker tape would thread its way from spools, up to the screen, and then down again on the floor. I was allowed to gather and wind around my finger as much used tape as I wanted. (One year, as a special treat, I was even given the end of a fresh spool.)

My grandfather and the other men would occasionally emit an emphatic *humph!* nod to each other, and then look up again at the screen. After twenty min-utes or so, they would pick up their straw hats and leave. I had no idea what was going on and didn't care; I was just too fascinated with the movement of the tape.

After going down on the elevator, we would walk over to the farmers' market. We visited my grandfather's favorite stalls and filled our wicker baskets with fresh bread, produce, and meat from Amish farmers. Then we were off to catch the West End bus to return home.

By sheer chance, I stayed overnight in downtown Lancaster recently. I was there to pick up my daughter from college and bring her home for winter break. Late in the evening, I took a walk three blocks down to the old square. The large five-and-ten had long since closed; many of the newer stores were much smaller and had the look of catering to the tourist trade, not the residents. The bank building was still there, although it had a bright logo sign of a large regional financial institution. In the dark, though, the square looked much the same as it did forty years ago. Yet, I knew it wasn't the same, and I wondered if any of the current customers of the bank ever recalled the old brokerage house on the top floor. Did anyone else retain a picture of old men sitting quietly, looking up at a lighted tape of letters and numbers? Was I the only one alive who remembered what happened up there?

I know that we live in an age when the familiar is being remodeled and the traditional obliterated. Maybe that is why I consider it important for me not to devalue memories. I hope my children will remember some of the places we have gone and things we have done together, even if they had not the slightest idea what was going on at the time. Benjamin Franklin said, in effect, that if we try to teach our children just what they will readily understand at the moment, we will produce remarkably feeble adults. Many things don't fall into place until years later.

Perhaps that is why it took so long for the Gospels to gel. They weren't simply the fuzzy reminiscences of old men and women. Some of them gathered Jesus' teachings and wove them together, like Matthew's Sermon on the Mount. Others, like Mark and Luke, thread various sayings and teachings throughout their Gospels. They digested some memories that made little sense at the time, but they came together later. When the pieces finally fell into place as a whole Gospel, then God's presence came into focus and a much larger and clearer view emerged. (If you are going to take the gospel seriously, you are going to have to chew on some things a while.)

That is why I hope there is someone like me, who will be taking a child or grandchild through the square on the way to the farmers' market. They will point up to the tall bank building across the street, and say, "I remember when they had mechanical ticker-tape machines, when stocks and bonds were traded with sound and movement, when fellow customers knew each other's names, and even a young boy who had no idea what fortunes were made or lost, who had no idea what a fortune was for that matter, was occasionally tolerated and allowed a souvenir connecting him to a large world beyond his immediate comprehension."

Jesus, Mustard Seeds, and Stomach Flu

He also said, "With what can we compare the kingdom of God, or what para-
ble will we use for it? It is like a mustard seed, which, when sown upon the
ground, is the smallest of all the seeds on earth; yet when it is sown it grows
up and becomes the greatest of all shrubs, and puts forth large branches, so
that the birds of the air can make nests in its shade."

Mark 4:30–32

I t is easy to forget that Jesus spent most of his earthly ministry in a small area among very modest sized communities. The Sea of Galilee is no more than fourteen miles long and eight miles across at its widest point, covering a surface area of sixty-four square miles—a small lake at best. If we made a comparison, I suspect we would find that most of us live near lakes that are larger. In the West, Lake Tahoe, for example, is twenty-six miles long and twelve miles wide, and in the East, Lake Champlain is one hundred seven miles long and fourteen miles at its widest, the same as Galilee's length. The local synagogues were virtually the only cultural centers in town but they were still very modest, not cathedral-like structures.

As children, whenever we drove through a small town that seemed down at its heels, we would exclaim, "This is a good town to be *from*." Of course, it is a thoughtless remark, but from a child it may be excused. Nonetheless, what we today would consider a small town is the kind of place Jesus came from and went to.

We can picture Jesus at a small unglamorous hamlet saying, "If you had faith the size of a mustard seed, you could say to this mulberry tree, 'Be uprooted and planted into the sea.'" At first it sounds preposterous. What Jesus seems to be saying to his listeners back then and to us is that even if we had the potential only a tenth the size of what Jesus knows we do have, we would still be able to do significant things in God's name. Even if our faith community were as small as the tiniest congregation in our district, our ministry would still be precious. A simple act of kindness is still an act of discipleship. The new commonwealth of God is as present among us here as it is anywhere else.

Then Jesus goes on to offer an analogy of a slave coming in from the field after a day's hard labor and serving his master dinner before he even thinks of eating himself. An unremarkable situation for people of the first century, it is completely foreign and offensive to us. Hence let me try to translate what Jesus was getting at. You came home a little late after a difficult day at the office. You rushed to prepare dinner and afterwards washed the dishes. Then you have helped your children, both of whom are cranky because they have a difficult math test tomorrow, with their homework. You have finally gotten them into bed and packed their lunches for tomorrow. If at three o'clock in the morning one of your children gets the stomach flu, which one of you would say to the child, "Hey, it's the middle of the night. I'm not paid to work overtime. I'm off duty as your parent now and I won't be back in service until I get up for breakfast"?

Rather, would you not get up, help clean up the mess and give some comfort to your child, who expresses thanks by getting sick again, all over you. That's what good parents do—take care of sick children at three o'clock in the morning. You don't expect a medal for it, do you?

What Jesus is getting at, of course, is that discipleship is not usually about answering big three-alarm fires. Discipleship is more like parenthood, where you are always on call but mostly for mundane things such as attending a recital, bandaging a skinned knee, or hosting a first-grade birthday party. Rather than putting on evening clothes to make an appearance, or putting on the firefighter's helmet to save the town hall, discipleship is more like putting on a bathrobe and getting a bucket.

We live in a society that scares us into thinking we have to accomplish something big and consequential or we will be left behind, and there will be nothing left for us. Our society tries to hold us in a perpetual fear of scarcity and inadequacy. Consequently we habitually feel that we are about to collapse.

The gospel, the Good News, says something different. It says, even if we have only half of what we think we have and wished we had, God will work with us. And when we share what we have, when we are open and generous, we inevitably make it through, we discover fresh resources, and what we have has been enhanced, not dissipated. We do not lose out when we take care of the more modest obligations. While it may seem like our children sometimes grow an inch a day, the route from childhood to maturity takes more small steps than giant strides.

It is a mystery. We always told our children, "When you feel you are getting sick, go to the bathroom, and then call Mommy and Daddy." Yet despite the darkness, they always passed by the bathroom and went straight to our bed instead. A greater mystery is how we found the energy to survive the stomach flu as our parents did for us when we got the chicken pox, measles, and mumps. On call, twenty-four hours a day. Yet we lived to tell, and to laugh, and even to look back on those times and say life was good. And those times were good!

All of which is to reiterate: ministry is significant, wherever and whenever it is done. Stomach flu afflicts us all. Thus mustard seeds and the precious ministry done in small towns are related.

Jesus the Shoe Salesman

"...And a woman named Martha welcomed him into her house. She had a sister named Mary who sat down at the Lord's feet and listened to him speaking."
Luke 10:39, The Jerusalem Bible

Picture a clerk at a shoe store with only one shoe box beside him. Kneeling in front of a customer, he is trying to squeeze on a pair of shoes. The customer is obviously determined to have this particular pair and the poor shoe salesman's frustration is equally obvious. This pair of shoes simply will not fit.

Now picture another scene in the shoe store. In contrast, the floor around the salesclerk is littered with dozens of boxes of shoes. The clerk is not hurrying to make a sale but carefully trying on the shoes and offering advice. The customer is at ease and trusts that the best fit will be found.

I would like to suggest that this story of Mary and Martha is not about one sister being pitted against another. Rather, it is about Jesus affirming both of them and giving them Good News that liberates them from their own particular bondage.

In Jesus' day it was unusual for the ordinary woman to receive much education beyond a rudimentary level. Rabbis conducted most of their classes for men. But Jesus was different. Jesus was an early advocate for coeducation, long before modern educators thought of it. Women were included among Jesus' closest disciples. Hence, Mary is welcomed into Jesus' circle and her choice is affirmed.

We know from other stories in Luke and John that Martha's house was a safe place for the disciples. Martha was a friend of Jesus, not a stranger, and Jesus felt comfortable there. We know very little about the exact circumstances, but Martha was obviously an independent and self-confident woman to tolerate a bunch of disciples hanging around her place. Like a true friend, Jesus is concerned about her, for she seems to be a very driven person whether by forces from within or from without. She seems, at times, to be practically captured by busyness.

We all know people who are too busy to pay attention to their families or to their own health. It is considerably more difficult to see the same situation in ourselves. We often assume that if we are busy, what we are doing is worthwhile. Often, though, our busyness simply covers up our emptiness and refusal to change. We continually run close to the edge of exhaustion. We fear all that we have is slipping away. We spin our wheels even faster, just as when the wheels of our car begin slipping on some winter ice and, in panic, we push the accelerator down to the floor. Usually it doesn't help, and we merely dig our tires deeper into a rut.

I wonder if Jesus doesn't say with a smile, "Martha, the boys can open their own wineskins. They know where the chips and salsa are. For heaven's sake, you're not entertaining the high priests from Jerusalem."

Jesus does not want Martha to be like Mary any more than Jesus wanted the Jewish lawyer who asked, "Who is my neighbor?" to become a Samaritan. Rather this story serves as an invitation to us to let the Good News be the Good News. For God, the one size of the world never fits all. Martha needed to know it was okay to have some space for herself. Jesus did not expect her to exhaust herself. Jesus wanted Martha to have an abundant life, a life open to the signs of God's grace. Martha's agenda was just too full: the load she was carrying was overwhelming her. She was so distracted she couldn't enjoy her own party with her friends. The better part for Mary was to slake her thirst for Jesus' teaching. The better part for Martha was to allow herself to be refreshed by Jesus' companionship.

In my spare time, I dream of designing stained-glass windows. I have yet to win a commission, but I understand that Michelangelo as a young man had to struggle, too. When I design Martha's window it will show Jesus as a shoe clerk in the mall, with boxes of shoes all around him. Jesus will be smiling and in no particular hurry as he tries on dozens of pairs on Martha's feet. You'll be able to tell that her anxiety is changing into trust; she is coming to understand that Jesus will find the right pair. The gospel offers the proper shoes for people of faith to walk in, and a fit that allows toes to wiggle and grow.

The Spirit of the Adirondacks and the Parable of the Talents

You have shown you can be faithful in small things, I will trust you with greater.

Matthew 25:21
The Jerusalem Bible

There was once an eccentric who, on one late October day, pulled into his neighbor's driveway in a large pickup truck. "Here," he said. "I'm going to Florida for the winter, but I have a hunch you are really going to get hit by snow this year." He unloaded a large self-propelled snow blower. "Keep it until I return," he said, as he jumped back into his truck, waved, and roared down the street.

Next, he pulled up to another neighbor's house. By the garage door, he deposited a hydraulic snow plow. "This size oughta fit your truck just fine," he yelled. "It will only take thirty minutes to bolt it on. The directions are taped to the front of the plow."

Again he left with a smile and wave, roaring off to a third neighbor's house, where he lifted out a brand new snow thrower. "Hi, neighbor," he said, "I saw your long winding flagstone walk. I'm going south soon, and I won't return till after Easter. It's full of gas and all checked out. Bye!"

It was an especially snowy winter in the North Country that year. Apparently the caterpillars grew two coats instead of one. But spring came at last, and sure enough, the first neighbor heard the distinctive sound of the large pickup truck as it drove up. "Hi, neighbor, how did it go?"

"Fine," replied the neighbor. "Thanks so much for your gift. The lady next door to us is quite elderly and after every snowstorm, I was able to clear her walk so she could get out to her mail box for eagerly awaited letters from her children and grandchildren."

"Hey, that's great! Keep the snow blower, and here's a coupon for a free tune-up at Agway."

Then he drove up to the second neighbor, beeping his horn. "Hey, how did the plow work?"

"Oh, it was a godsend," said the second neighbor, "especially when we had the blizzard that dumped thirty-six inches in six hours. I was able to plow the driveways of three of my neighbors. One had a bad back, another just had an operation, and the third worked at the hospital and would not have gotten to work if I hadn't had your plow."

"Wonderful!" came the reply. "Why don't you keep it for next year, and by the way, here is a pair of new snow tires for your truck. When you use that plow you want good traction." Then he sped off to the third neighbor.

"Well, you need not have worried," said the neighbor when he saw the truck. "Your snow thrower is safe in my shed. I know how much I resent lending things for my neighbors to use, especially things that cost me a pretty penny. I would get pretty steamed if this snow thrower were mine and some fool broke the shear pin or chipped the paint, so I never even started it up. It's in exactly the same condition that you left it."

"You fool," replied the eccentric. "This past winter was the snowiest winter on record in the North Country and you never even started it. I might as well take it back and give it to the guy I gave the plow to down the street."

Jesus was telling us in the parable of the talents that God is even more lavish than the eccentric in the pickup truck. Even one talent would be the equivalent of approximately eighteen hundred dollars, and that was back in the days when a thousand dollars would buy a lot of farm implements! God is generous, but some don't accept it. They project their own personality of meanness and hardness on God, and that projection just comes back to hit them in the face.

God has given us many gifts. Not all exactly the same, but many, many gifts. Yes, we can be resentful that we won only a hundred dollars in the state lottery and someone in Buffalo always wins the big jackpot. We can be jealous that a neighbor, a relative, or even a church down the street has a bigger income than ours. Such walls of resentment prevent us from appreciating God's generosity and the potential use and opportunity for the many gifts we have.

We have all the resources we need to participate in the mission God gives us, wherever we are. The question the parable asks is, are we willing to use and to share them? What is a snow blower for? To be stored in a shed? Of course not. Is the worst thing that can happen to a snow blower a broken shear pin? Isn't it a far more foolish thing to be afraid to start the snow blower and use it in the first place?

Jesus doesn't ask disciples to keep themselves clean from the messes and brokenness of the world but to help in cleaning the wounds and healing the injuries. Christians are those who start the snow blowers, getting their fingernails dirty with oil and gasoline, clearing paths in the night when visibility is nil. Jesus doesn't want a clean balance sheet as much as he wants us to leverage our gifts for the healing of humanity.

There is an old saying in the Adirondacks that anyone in need of help need only to call out, and people of good will leave their work and home and come running.[1] It rings true. Sometimes people ask me, "Do you really think people could be as eccentric and generous as some of the examples in Jesus' parables?" "Yes," I reply, "I have lived in the North Country, and I have met them."

---

1. William Chapman White, *Adirondack Country* (Syracuse, N.Y.: Syracuse University Press, 1985), p. v.

Yield House and the North Conway Railway Express Office

Do not presume to say to yourselves, "We have Abraham as our ancestor"; for I tell you, God is able from these stones to raise up children to Abraham.
Matthew 3:9

Last week, one of my sons saw that I was watching *Antiques Roadshow*, a TV program where anyone can bring in a treasure and an appraiser will give an indication of its age and value. Afterward he pointed to a record cabinet and said with dollar signs in his eyes, "Is that an antique?"

"No," I replied. "It isn't." In fact, it was a kit I put together to take to college. It came from North Conway, New Hampshire, from a modest place called Yield House, which sold genuine pine furniture. Long before the day of twenty-four-hour toll-free calls and colorful catalogs, my order was picked up at the store, taken to the North Conway railroad station, and shipped by rail to Albany. In two to three weeks, a dark green Railway Express Agency truck delivered it to my house.

The Railway Express Agency was the way most large parcels and personal merchandise were moved. The company was owned by the railroads, and wherever there was a working station, the REA was set up to accept and deliver duffel bags to summer camps and anything in the Wards or Sears catalog to their customers. When passenger trains were cut and stations consolidated or abandoned, the Railway Express Agency also cut back. With the virtual death of train service in most communities, the Railway Express Agency went bankrupt.

Yield House, on the other hand, expanded by leaps and bounds. It developed a national catalog and opened several retail outlets. It still ships its items from North Conway, but now the orders are picked up and driven to Boston, transported by plane, and delivered by a truck operated by Federal Express, a huge multinational corporation.

REA would be going today and FedEx unknown if REA had done one simple thing: moved its terminals from the railroad stations to the airports. REA had the expertise, the organization, and the franchise in every community. REA didn't go bankrupt because the shippers or customers went away and demand went down. FedEx didn't invent some amazing technology; actually, they probably cloned REA's. But REA thought it was welded to the railroad business, and all the time it was really in the transportation business. That is the reason the first morning a delivery truck left Yield House and turned right to Boston instead of left to the station, it was a momentous (if ironically a hardly noticed) event.

Matthew, Mark, and Luke all report Jesus' rejection in his hometown synagogue of Nazareth, an important turning point in his ministry. When Jesus is kicked out of the synagogue and shouted down by his neighbors, he initiates a new type of mission, independent of synagogue and family connections. Jesus bypasses two of the most powerful institutions of his society and trains disciples and sends them out to deliver the Good News of God.

Jesus' mission is not to preach in every synagogue but to preach the gospel. Jesus is called not to be a rabbi with a local reputation but to be the savior of the world. Mark is reminding us that the church must continually ask what God calls it to be and refocus its mission. God is always able to bypass what we might consider the usual ways and proper channels. Complacency is hazardous for people of God. Any group of Christians that forgets that will become as quaint as the old express wagons with large steel wheels that hold flowers or wine bottles at those ubiquitous theme restaurants.

Christians are not the Historic Liturgy Association, or the Society for the Preservation of Tall Steeples, or the reorganized Friends of Copes, Crooks, and Chasubles. The people of God are gospel proclaimers, witnesses to Christ's resurrection. Unlike the Railway Express Agency, we are not welded to one means of delivery, or one color of truck, or a particular station's location.

One of the most powerful images in the prophets is of Amos and the vision of the plumb line. "I see a plumb line," Amos announces. He continues, fearlessly condemning the king and high priest with the words, "Then the LORD said: See, I am setting a plumb line in the midst of my people: I will never again pass them by; the high places of Isaac shall be made desolate and the sanctuaries of Israel shall be made waste" (Amos 7:7–9, Jerusalem Bible). No doubt there are many churches that incorporate Amos's plumb line into their iconography. But I wonder if for us today a diagonal REA sign might be equally provocative.

Renewal: Things Too Good to Leave Behind

You are the salt of the earth.... You are the light of the world.
Matthew 5:13–14

Some twenty years ago, my spouse Kluane and I spent a three-day holiday in downtown Cleveland. Why Cleveland? It was on a lark really, the result of a feature article in the *New York Times* travel section. At the time Cleveland seemed to be on the edge of a renaissance.

The city now boasted a marvelous theater that had just been renovated; a landmark of a gilded age that had been turned into a plush restaurant; a mall with several levels framed in classic iron grills and railings, and intricate skylights reminiscent of the famous 1890s' Crystal Palace at Chicago's Columbian Exposition; and an interesting development project of small shops and a park along the river. Moreover, a short ride on the transit system brought one to the Cleveland Art Museum, which at the time was showing a fascinating exhibit on the European vision of America.

We boarded Amtrak in Albany at night. In those days, the sleeping cars were truly leftover orphans of dying railroads, and it was rare that the lights, plumbing, and air-conditioning all worked. It was not at all unusual for the attendant to switch you out of your assigned room to another where at least two out of the three operated. I remember that in our original room, the berths would not come down, but after being reassigned, the ride wasn't bad at all and we arrived in the morning on time. We disembarked on a temporary platform next to a rental construction trailer serving as a combination ticket office and four-chair waiting room near Cleveland's waterfront.

Our hotel was a product of a renewal project, not an ostentatious corporate convention center, but reasonably comfortable. From the window of our room on one of the upper floors we saw parking lots, a few buildings ready for demolition, an adult bookstore, and the skyline of the center city within walking distance.

"You've come to Cleveland for a holiday?" responded a smiling police officer when we asked for directions. "We were really written up in the Sunday *Times*? I can't believe it." The theater we had read about was every bit a mirrored pleasure house. It was neat walking along the largely open shoreline of Lake Erie, where yachts and large sailboats were moored. We walked by one of the tall ships scheduled to sail into New York harbor in Operation Sail on July 4, 1976. Out at the museum, the exhibit of the European vision of America created a thought-provoking and curious juxtaposition. In a fifteen-minute transit ride, we went from industrialized, urban America to a new world, depicted on large canvases, with tremendous waterfalls and deep forests populated by surreal creatures of fifteenth- and sixteenth-century European imagination. Come to think of it, parts of what would become the real industrialized America were even more surreal and scary than some of the apocalyptic visions of Old World artists.

But the big surprise was in the area called the Flats, next to the twisting Cuyahoga River, before it empties into the lake. Immigrants, many of them Irish, first landed on the Flats hoping to find work in Cleveland's factories. Like similar areas in many a city, this stopping place on the road to a better life became a dismal shanty- and rooming-house town, interspersed with grimy warehouses. By the 1950s the Flats was an industrial slum, full of forgotten junkyards, deserted shells of buildings, and rotting piers. The river became so polluted that its surface ignited and damaged several bridges.

Perhaps there was also an alarm that sounded in people's memory. For by the river, near the spot it caught fire, we found Settlers Landing Park, a delightful acre of green. Next door in a restored brick warehouse were two shops, one filled with handmade linens and carvings made by Irish craftsmen and one with equally fine items from Poland. The proprietor of Emerald in the Flats, Mrs. Flynn, told us, "We came down here because this is where our people first landed, and we wanted to show others the beautiful things our forbears had to temporarily leave behind when they came to America." I can't recall what, if anything, we bought there, but I think Mrs. Flynn gave us something more precious than what we could afford to purchase.

We concluded our visit to the Flats by eating at one of the several riverfront restaurants that had also moved down there. Soon we were on Amtrak again, and returned home full of good things to say about Cleveland.

The years have passed, and for Cleveland the renaissance was postponed as it went through some very rough times. The tall ship moored at the waterfront was later lost at sea. They've built a new stadium and the Rock and Roll Hall of Fame, but we've never returned.

Undoubtedly, Mrs. Flynn has long since retired, but I'd like to think her shop has continued and the brave venture at the Flats has succeeded. For if any community is to be renewed, it will be through the Mrs. Flynns of the world, who affirm in the present what is too good to leave behind, and who forge the future with their courage.

Jesus said, "You are the salt of the earth. You are the light of the world." Note Jesus didn't say, "You are to sprinkle a little salt around your small group of friends." Or, "You are to be a light, flickering inside of a tight little community." Rather, you are to season the whole earth, you are to be a light of God's grace in the world. People of faith are practitioners of the ripple effect. They are like fireflies on a summer's night, carrying a light over great distances, letting it shine here and there, until it is almost automatic.

It was probably on a hillside overlooking the lake of Galilee or in a synagogue in one of the fishing villages along its shore that Jesus first said, "You are salt of the earth; you are the light of the world." But when I think about those words, I don't picture the usual pastoral scene of people in robes and sandals. Instead I think of Mrs. Flynn, founder and proprietor of Emerald in the Flats, on the banks of the Cuyahoga River.

No Fries in Maine

From his fullness we have all received grace upon grace.
John 1:16

While on vacation along the Maine seacoast one summer, we purposely tried to stop at the small local eateries along the back roads. They were definitely not fast food. No one asked, after we gave our order, *"Do you want fries with that?"* The service was sometimes slow, but most were places of genuine hospitality. Preparing lunch or dipping a large ice cream cone was not simply an economic transaction, it also became a brief but genuine sharing of a special grace. Whenever I travel, I remember the unexpected kindness, the unassuming pleasantness, or the spontaneous and helpful favor of a total stranger the most.

Jesus uses the theme of hospitality as a way to compare the way of God with the conventions of the world. The social etiquette of the world is inevitably concerned with proper places, obtaining all that is due, squeezing every opportunity to one's advantage, always asking, *"Do you want fries with that?"*

Jesus was not without a sense of humor, even when talking about serious things. That becomes evident in the Gospel where Jesus notices how concerned guests are over their seating. Jesus realizes that he is around people who want to discuss and negotiate their way into God's good graces, who are anxious about their status, but who don't necessarily want to commit themselves to any vision of new life. They wish to argue over how many will be saved. They are concerned about who will sit where and how they can build up credits on their charge cards to apply to the heavenly banquet. So Jesus says, "Hey, don't worry about where you sit when you are invited to a banquet. Your worry will just overwhelm and spoil the happy occasion for you. The same food is served at all places. There are forks at every place. Relax and enjoy yourselves, savor the company of whoever sits next to you. If the host wants to put you at the head table, Hah! You will be singled out and praised in front of everyone."

Then Jesus realizes how easily we can twist things around. I wonder if Jesus may have thought, Uh, oh. I see it now. People rushing to the last chairs just like the last pews in church, fighting over the lowest place, out-humbling themselves so that they can get recognized and get a higher place.

So Jesus tries again. Don't worry about how one party will gain you a ticket into an even better party. Just enjoy the party at hand. When you give a party, instead of thinking what benefit it will bring you, give a party for those who will enjoy it as a gift. Don't expect anything more out of it except that people will have a good time. So don't invite to supper those who are sure to reciprocate and maybe even invite you to a fancier meal. Even if you use the White House cookbook, do you think you can put on a spread to outdo the heavenly banquet?

Now Jesus is not against planning, but often we let lesser concerns and arguments obscure our understanding of a greater world. Our spiritual energy becomes short-circuited and drained. Yet citizens of the commonwealth of God don't need to worry about who will sit where or about how God will settle up.

We may give merely as we think others deserve, but Jesus emphasizes God's generosity and genuine open-armed welcome to us all. That is why, I suspect, as in the small unpretentious villages along the coast of Maine, there are no fast-food places planned to be built in God's new world.

Discovering Heydays

Since then, we have such a hope, we act with great boldness…. So we do not lose heart… because we look not at what can be seen but at what cannot be seen.

2 Corinthians 3:12; 4:16, 18

I am obviously an inveterate railroad fan, and it's a real treat for me to drive out from the city and along some three-digit county road to discover the foundations of an old passenger station. It's fun to spend a summer's afternoon in fields of milkweed and goldenrod, figuring out where all the sidings were and where the steam lines ran to heat the cars in winter and dreaming about the years when dozens of trains used to stop there. At some sites, the walls of the water tower and coal bins are still standing, and in a few of the back places of the Adirondacks, the bank of outhouses is still intact and usable. As I poke around, sounds of whistles, announcements, and greetings of passengers come easily to the imagination. It's great to drink a cold soda while sitting on the bed of a steel-tired baggage cart, wondering what year and day it was when the last trunk was taken off and the cart pushed into the clump of young sumac bushes. The first half of the twentieth century was the heyday of railroad passenger travel, and how I wish I could bring it back.

It's a harmless fantasy, but a fantasy nonetheless. The tracks have been torn up, and no train will go by there ever again. After a while, I have to get back into my car and return home. There will be messages to answer and obligations to assume. If I need to go to New York or Chicago next week, I won't think of the old abandoned rail line at all but will drive to the airport and take a plane.

It's tempting to think of what parish life was like in days gone by. Healthy as it may be to hold on to and savor good memories, it's problematic to let memories indiscriminately grip us by the throat. It's easy to relinquish reality and repeat as a mantra, "In the church's heyday, Christians received the energy to take the gospel to all nations and translate the Good News into the language and culture of varied people. In the church's heyday, Christians preserved much of the wisdom of Roman and Greek civilization. In its heyday, Christians took care of people who were stricken with bubonic plague. In its heyday, Christians hid Jews from the Nazis. In its heyday, great cathedrals were filled with crowds of people every Sunday."

Today, more feeding programs are housed in churches than at any time in our nation's history; more Christians are working to solve the problem of homelessness than ever before in the history of the National Council of Churches; and more people are concerned about the environment of the earth than at any time in this century. Physicians are leaving their practices and clergy are resigning from parish responsibilities to go and minister to those afflicted with AIDS. In the church's heyday, people respond to the Good News and carry the love of Christ out to feed the hungry, to care for the sick, and to act as good stewards of the earth. When we connect the gospel with what God calls us to do this week, we get plugged in to the church's heyday of yesterday, today, and tomorrow. When people heed the call of God, the Spirit is born again, the journey continues forward, and the church works out its salvation in the world. It is God who is at work in us; God who changes our minds, adjusts our directions, and helps us hold on to memories without their keeping us in a wilderness of ruined foundations and rotting outhouses.

Yes, in the heyday of passenger trains, every hamlet of three dozen habitations seemed to have its own railroad station, serviced daily by a handful of trains. But we live in our own heyday, and we travel by different means. There was a heyday of different church structures and ways of operation than we have now, and it is okay to travel down back roads of reminiscences as long as tears for the past don't prevent us from finding our way back to our home. It's still the heyday for people of faith.

The University Club

And know that I am with you always; yes, to the end of time.
> Matthew 28:20
> The Jerusalem Bible

During August, it is customary for my spouse and me to spend some time with my mother in Albany, in the house I grew up in, doing painting and other light repairs. One of the rewards is going out to eat at the end of the day. We inevitably go to a venerable Albany institution a few blocks from the capitol—a place where I have been taken since I was a child—and are seated at our usual table. Although it has undoubtedly been redecorated many times, the dining room still looks exactly the same as it did in the fifties. Winter landscapes by a painter of the Hudson River School hang on the walls, where they have for decades; the red upholstery on the dining room chairs is the same. Some would call the place stodgy, but even in its formality I always found it comforting. It seems like an old friend who has never changed and welcomes you back as if you had never left.

Once when we were eating at the club, just finishing our appetizer, a man walked in. I would have known who he was even if the hostess had not greeted him by name. I hadn't seen him for at least twenty years and probably hadn't had a real conversation with him in thirty. He was my seventh-grade history teacher, who was also the school's football, basketball, and baseball coach. Known as a strict teacher and demanding coach, he was also scrupulously fair and straightforward.

I went over and introduced myself to him, and he seemed genuinely glad to see me. After dinner, we gathered and talked. "You were in the class of 1964, right?" he said, emphasizing that he had not forgotten me. As he filled me in very quickly on all that had gone on in the school before he retired, I began to realize that we were talking as adults, not as pupil and teacher. He didn't seem to remember me as a shy and painfully awkward seventh grader. Perhaps what made him a successful coach and a well-loved teacher was that he never did see his charges for what they were, but for what they could and would become. He was demanding, for he believed in their potential and fully expected them to grow into it. He knew most of our lives would be spent as adults, not as adolescents. As we said good-bye, I hoped that it wouldn't be so long until I saw him again. His face brought back good memories. What I didn't say, but reflected on in the weeks after and wished he could know, was that I have never forgotten him. True, I hadn't consciously thought of him in years, but he was still with me.

Jesus was willing to eat with just about anyone. On any given day, he was as likely to eat with financiers and lawyers at a lavish banquet as with itinerants at their camp along the lake shore. We have stories of Jesus eating with rich and powerful hosts who seem to be very conscious of, if not outright anxious about, maintaining and hopefully enhancing their social standing. Jesus realized that those with whom he was eating were likely to have been pretty shrewd investors, those who were skillful at evaluating and planning. Yet, Jesus knew that those he ate with were capable of much, much more. Their notion of hospitality was painfully underdeveloped. Jesus taught them, expecting them to grow into a larger vision of hospitality, a vision formed by God. God's hospitality is not the same as seeking or planning a strategy for a decent return. That is why if we think Jesus is saying to us, "A way to score extra credits with God is to get humble, slight your family and friends, and invite all the poor to a picnic; the more poor you feed, the more bonus points you earn," we are missing the point entirely.

In cooking you can often use substitute ingredients: margarine in place of butter, or granulated sugar and a pinch of cornstarch in place of powdered sugar, or baking soda and cream of tartar in place of baking powder. But hospitality has no such substitutes. Hospitality basically means love of stranger. Like all love, you can't substitute money—or anything else for that matter—in place of it. Like good teaching, hospitality is unique. You can't fake the real thing.

God intends hospitality to be offered with no strings attached, with no subtle overtones of control or influence. Hospitality is not offered as barter for something else. In God's commonwealth, of course, God is the host and we are the guests. Disciples are those who let others know that they too are invited, as we are. Disciples are those who believe that there is still growth in each of us.

Because such stories of Jesus at meals have been remembered and written down, it appears that some of those who ate with him did not forget him, that he was still with them even after many years. I would like to think that some became disciples and that some did indeed grow into their potential to offer a hospitality informed by the vision of God.

The Route of the Laurentian

Are you the one who is to come, or are we to wait for another?
                                                        Luke 7:19

Back in the days when railroads were proud of their passenger trains, the pride of the Delaware and Hudson Railroad was the Laurentian, running between New York City and Montreal. The journey, known for its beautiful scenery, ran along the east shore of the Hudson River and then along the west shore of Lake Champlain. Unfortunately, the D & H was squeezed between much larger railroads and for the first half of its route, it ran on the tracks of foreign territory, coupled with a train of the New York Central. Pulled by the Central's engines, it was not until Albany, where the New York Central broke off and headed west to Chicago, that the D & H took control of its own train and coupled on its sleek silver and blue diesels. The engines were real beauties, unlike the homely designs of many in that era of the 1950s. They were built in Schenectady and looked like long proud greyhounds, with strong angular noses.

After leaving Albany and passing Saratoga, they headed northeast to Lake Champlain, where they twisted and curved around its shore. There were spectacular views for the passengers, but the engines always had to hold back and keep braking for the tight curves. (The passengers didn't want their coffee or soup spilled, either.) After the train passed Plattsburgh, nearly at the end of its journey, and came into the broad plain of the St. Lawrence Valley, the engineer could operate at full throttle and the engines finally could run as they were intended, bounding all the way into Montreal.

Many people dread the world's holiday season because they are constantly told to cheer up and they don't feel like that at all. Indeed the road they face looks pretty twisted and confusing. Advent is a gift because it reminds us that the broad, smooth, and unobstructed highways of faith are the glorious ideal and the exception. Most of our roads of faith are rather narrow and hilly, and sometimes are so poorly marked that we are none too sure we have found the way. Often we seem to wander into alien territory. Instead of running at full throttle, we spend our time struggling to put one foot in front of the other and sometimes using our hands to grab hold, too.

Advent helps us to ponder the meaning of the story of John the Baptist sending word from prison and asking Jesus, "Are you the one who is to come?" Why did Matthew and Luke include it in their Gospels? One possible answer is that they wanted us to know that John had doubts and questions just as we do, and he was not rebuked for them. Nor was John told to look for the broad highways or suddenly disappearing mountains or other spectacular wonders on a grand scale. "The poor have good news preached to them," came back the reply. John was told to look for signs—signs of healing among the sick, signs of new life among those considered dead or those considered outcast. John was told to look for signs of God's presence among all the troubled and twisted back alleys of the world.

I suspect that the original purpose of an Advent wreath with candles is related to the same reason people put extra lights on their houses this time of year: it's dark outside and it is going to get darker before it gets lighter. The Advent wreath is there to provide more light, one candle at a time. No spectacular fireworks. The wreath doesn't deny the darkness; nonetheless, it is a sign that light exists.

The official explanation of why the third candle on the Advent wreath is a different color than the others is that the opening verses and responses originally used on the third Sunday in Advent urged people to rejoice and lift up their hearts, for the Lord was near. Hence, instead of the more somber color of violet, the vestments were changed to a lighter, more joyful color called rose.

However, I would offer a completely unofficial explanation for why one candle is a different color. I wonder if right before a service began during this dark season of the year, a congregation discovered they had only three large candles that matched. Since the purpose of the candles wasn't that they be the same, but only that they give light in the darkness, people found another candle and wisely used it. Rather than resign themselves in despair and cancel the service, they made do with what they had. That in itself became a sign of how the light of Christ works among us.

All of which is to say that the season of Advent speaks to those whose lives are *not* the broad easy highway of ho ho ho's. It speaks of God's presence coming among us, one step at a time, sometimes more slowly than we would like. It speaks of signs among prisoners, among the ill, among the unpleasant things the world would never mention in its holiday celebration.

The D & H Railroad has been swallowed up. A few shields of the company's logo, rusting away on some scattered upstate bridges, are the last vestiges of this independent and spiffy railroad line. The very few remaining locomotives, once built at the American Locomotive Works in Schenectady, are museum pieces. Yet I still think that Advent is a lot like the once daily journey of a plucky little train known as the Laurentian.

Routine and Relics

It is the same God that said, "Let there be light shining out of darkness," who has shone in our minds to radiate the light of the knowledge of God's glory, the glory on the face of Christ. We are only the earthenware jars that hold this treasure, to make it clear that such an overwhelming power comes from God and not from us.

2 Corinthians 4:6–7
The Jerusalem Bible

Decorating for Christmas at our house was always a serious matter. There was a definite routine to things and if I or my younger sister, much less my parents, ever strayed from it, objections would be raised. The crèche would be placed on the same cherry drop leaf table; the tree, in the same spot in the living room. A string of bubble lights would go on first at the top, then the regular lights, then the special bulbs, and so on. Last, the tinsel, the kind cut from lead shavings, would be hung in long strands. A mirror covered with flaked asbestos snow would go in front, with a few pine cone figures and green brush pine trees. Before we placed the presents around, I would crawl under the tree and look up at a fairy-land forest of color and light revealing itself. All was right with the world. In the kitchen, cookies would be made from old family recipes. There was always fussing about this recipe being too buttery and about how it was very difficult to find rose water without glycerin again this year; nonetheless, the recipes would never be revised. Tradition had to be satisfied.

The other day, I was cleaning out a drawer and found several Christmas carol song booklets. Most had a picture of a large cut-stone church, illuminated at night with snow falling around it, on the front cover. The booklets were printed by the millions and distributed by agents of the John Hancock Insurance Company. It was obviously good advertising. I recalled that no one ever taught me the words to Christmas carols. Numerous community groups had sings and tree lightings, and it was by osmosis of my culture—not intentional effort by family or parish church—that I learned those songs by heart. I also realized that in holding the booklets, I was holding a relic of the past.

No longer is it in good taste for a large company to publish millions of Christmas carol booklets. You may hear the tunes, but increasingly rarely do you hear the words to the true carols. In the public schools, Christmas concerts have become holiday concerts, and Christmas break has become midwinter recess. It is still hard to accept that Christians have in a real sense lost control of the surrounding culture. My grandchildren will have to be taught the words to "Silent Night."

I suppose much of the tradition of decorating was a form of childhood control. I don't take it so seriously anymore and after I was married I discovered my spouse, not to mention my own children, had ideas very different from my own. I don't doubt that is all to the good. And over the years, a healthy equilibrium has been established.

I wonder if the season of Advent might be a real gift to us at this juncture. Advent is a season of waiting, but it is also a reminder that we never have the control we think we do. Mary and Joseph leave Nazareth for Bethlehem, unsure what exactly is in store but having a sense that things will never be the same. Certainly the arrival of shepherds and magi and the reports of angels singing in fields are unnerving and confirm that their lives are *in process*. The magi leave for home on a different route, and the holy family leaves for Egypt knowing they will be living in a land very different from what they have experienced.

I still cherish tradition and I am not sorry for all those customs of the past. But I know that Advent, a period of waiting when we acknowledge that change and unexpectedness is part of the game, has helped me celebrate Christmas with more maturity. For within the Christmas story of new births and beginnings is also the recurring theme of taking leave and letting go, of looking beyond the horizon, and of being open to surprise.

Expedition for Balsam

I am about to do a new thing; now it springs forth, do you not perceive it? I will make a way in the wilderness and rivers in the desert.
Isaiah 43:19

One of my favorite memories of living in the Adirondacks is going out into the woods every December before Christmas in search of a stand of a dozen balsam fir trees to decorate the church. Several parishioners owned land that we could scout on, and balsams grow like weeds in the northern Adirondacks. A small group of us would split up and soon each would be in the forest alone. At some point I would stop and just look around and become aware of the immense silence. After a few minutes, I might hear the chattering of a few birds or a soft drip of snow melting off the pine needles. I knew even my bodily systems were calming down and enjoying the respite.

I left the mountains of northern New York over ten years ago and have learned to restrain my passion for fresh balsam. I've had a comparable experience, though, when late on a cold night, I've taken the garbage can down my driveway to the road. By the time I am halfway back, my eyes have adjusted. When I look up, I am able to see blinking satellites, bright planets, and thousands of stars, and I have a profound sense of being surrounded in the quiet darkness.

Now neither did the woods begin their silence and icicles begin to drip at the moment I ventured out from town, nor did the stars appear in the sky as I was walking down the driveway. Rather, because I allowed my senses both space and time to adjust, because I was willing to leave a warm house or car and walk into the woods, or walk away from the street lights and raise my head to the sky, I was prepared to enjoy the silence of winter, hear the small voices of birds, and admire the Milky Way. But those things were present all the time.

In the same way, while Advent is a season of preparation, Christmas does not arrive among us because we have prepared. The secular world would like us to believe that it just would not be Christmas if we didn't bake those fruitcakes, send the cards, and mail out pounds of gifts. Nonsense! Rather we prepare because God promises to be among us. Christmas will arrive. Nothing will prevent it, not even a UPS strike or a computer shut-down at L.L. Bean. God's birth in this world can be counted on, and that's the reason we prepare and make room.

Periods of profound upheaval and change were commonplace for those who lived in the centuries before and after Jesus. One of the first shocks for Christians was the destruction of Jerusalem in the year 70. Matthew, Mark, and Luke all reflect this event, albeit in subtle and different ways. Although it happened well after the Resurrection, the establishment of the early church, and the larger mission to the Gentile world, the devastation of this city, holy to both Jew and Christian, was cataclysmic. It was tempting to draw back, to become cynical and disillusioned. The Gospel writers wanted their readers to know that this is just part of the picture. Yes, there have been and will be earthshaking things, but God is still in charge. God's new earth means the healing of the nations, the healing of nature. It means unimaginable reconciliation. God has made an immense commitment, and that's why the worries of this life, even events that threaten the foundations of our cultural and political institutions, will not prevent the presence of God in our world.

For Advent, the church offers us images of fig trees sprouting leaves, of dead stumps coming alive with shoots, of dry bones rising up and being joined together and transformed into a living community, of families, against all odds, being gathered together after generations of exile. We are all invited to unclog the hard drive of our senses, to stretch our minds, to empty our agendas, and to give our souls plenty of space to hope. There are all sorts of ways to do these things of course. One or two ways don't fit all.

Advent calendars are wonderfully clever yet simple things, aren't they? You open one small door every day, and at the end of Advent you have two dozen doors open, all ready to accept the Good News. That's the message of Advent. God is coming near, new birth is about to take place. Now is the time to open our gates, to remove obstructions in our way, to clear a path. It is the time to prepare our senses, our minds, our souls.

I know that by the beginning of November, the woods of the northern Adirondacks will soon be at rest again even if I never get to walk in them again. I know the Milky Way is always there. But when I'm rushing to get to home on time to dinner or to a vestry meeting, it's easy to forget. Christmas is often the rediscovery of the mystery of God's presence that has been among us all the time.

Toy Trucks and Treasure

The kingdom of heaven is like treasure hidden in a field, which someone found and hid; then in his joy he goes and sells all that he has and buys that field.
                                                                    Matthew 13:44

There were two important retail establishments that shaped my childhood. The most important was Charles Klarsfeld & Sons, which originally began as a bicycle shop but by the 1950s was *the* Lionel train store of Albany. Located on a narrow sloping side street, deep in the center city, it was a mecca for young and old. Its shelves held a collection fit for a model railroad tycoon. If Lionel and American Flyer ever built it, Klarsfeld had it displayed.

The second store was of lesser importance especially as I got older, but when I was about five or six a visit to view its merchandise was like a trip to the circus. It was called Silverstein's Toy Store, situated on Central Avenue in a newer, brighter section of town. While it carried toys of all descriptions, its specialty was large metal trucks, not dinky matchbox things or overpriced so-called collector's items that gas stations palm off at Christmas time, but solid toy trucks for real kids, large scale, a foot or more in length, with rubber tires, working steering mechanisms, doors that opened and slammed, and dumpers that dumped.

Silverstein's had a fleet of dozens, all on shelves along a long wall for children and their parents to admire.

As a young child, I was lucky enough to be given at least three: an orange Allis Chalmers earthmover, a fire engine pumper with ladder and hoses that connected to the garden hose and squirted a stream of water fifteen feet or more, and an army truck complete with cloth canopy and pulling a howitzer trailer. My friends and I played and played with them, until I graduated to trains. Near the end, I suppose, knowing that I was going into trains, I had a strange inclination to take the trucks apart, first the tires, then the doors and the chrome, and soon there was nothing left but a chassis and a pile of interesting small castings. Perhaps one or two did somehow make it to the church white elephant table, but by that time I was fully into trains and had left childish trucking behind forever.

These days, I occasionally see at antique shows one of those toy trucks of the 50s, shiny and new as they were when they were first under my Christmas trees. They still catch my eye. When I look and find that they are now selling for hundreds of dollars, I wish I hadn't been so hasty and had kept one or two intact. Yet maybe not. Maybe the five-year-old kid did the wise thing. That earthmover of mine moved tons of dirt and pretty near built the whole New York State Thruway. The army truck carried hundred of soldiers and equipment and the fire truck put out many a fire, hosing down the maple trees and making many a mud puddle in the front lawn. My friends and I got more than our money's worth out of them. That is why I'm not really sorry I didn't just save them in their original box and never take them outside to play. Yes, they'd be worth a pretty penny now, but on balance I would have more than lost out.

On the other hand, I'm glad to see others in antique shows at high prices. For it means that those that were never sold and enjoyed by a happy child, those that were forgotten in some carton, are now appreciated and bring enjoyment to collectors, perhaps even as much enjoyment to collectors as to those of us who worked them hard up and down the driveway.

Jesus offered many parables about the commonwealth of God. Parables were everyday stories meant to illustrate one or two points. They weren't meant to have extensive hidden meanings or to be some sort of comprehensive explanation of the full range of God's actions. The person who found the treasure in a field, and was so overjoyed that he sold everything to purchase the field, is not meant to get us discussing ethical questions such as "Should not the person have told the original owner of the field about the treasure?" or "Is the finder obligated to pay income tax on what he found?" We are dealing with a parable, not a case statement from Harvard Business School. The point is that the person realizes this great treasure is right before him; it is a gift that just dropped into his lap, and he gleefully responds and celebrates. "Look what has turned up!" he exclaims. He knows it is beyond what he would ordinarily ever find or obtain. He knows what he can do is be thankful. The story of the merchant who found the precious pearl makes the same point. The merchant realizes how valuable this pearl is. He cannot help but be overjoyed.

Part of being a community is recognizing the gifts that drop into our laps, acknowledging the talents and the workings of the spirit manifest among us and saying, "Wow, isn't that fine!" (That's all that a five-year-old child can do when given a super truck, just say "Wow!") The so-called secret of God's commonwealth isn't that we've searched and searched until we've found it, or that we've suffered and suffered long enough for God to take pity on us, or that we've played and played the lottery until we've just been lucky. Rather, the gifts of God's grace are often handed to us like seeds and when they are planted, they spring up and produce an incredible harvest.

God's gifts are like treasures found in the field, like pearls beyond price that just suddenly come our way, and like the toy trucks at Silverstein's Toy Store on Central Avenue that appear under the Christmas tree. People of faith know that God's gifts are meant to be discovered, appreciated, used, and enjoyed.

The Lights Along Highway 147

By the tender mercy of our God, the dawn from on high will break upon us, to give light to those who sit in darkness and in the shadow of death, to guide our feet into the way of peace.

Luke 1:78–79

We usually spend Christmas in our own home. But after Christmas, we go off for a week and share the season with parents and our extended family. So after the presents are unwrapped, admired, and stacked around the tree, we prepare to head south. One year, on the way to Baltimore from Ithaca on the day after Christmas, we took a back route, far removed from the interstate, and followed the Susquehanna River down to Harrisburg, Pennsylvania. The route is obviously an old one, for at one point, beautiful sycamore trees form a narrow arbor for several miles over what must have once been a one-lane track. It was evening as we passed through a half-dozen small towns and hamlets that were narrowly squeezed between the railroad and river on the right and heavily wooded cliffs on the left. In daylight, these places seem rather drab, having seen better days when they serviced railroad locomotives or when the ferry across the river was an important commercial link. Yet as we passed through, the little towns were all lit up as fairylands, with decorations along the four-block Main Streets and scenes on the modest village squares. The majority of houses joined in witnessing to the season. It was a happy surprise, and it reminded me that for Christians, Christmas is not a one-day celebration, over in twenty-four hours, but is a season. "Christmas is not over," those lights from Pennsylvania river towns proclaimed to all who anonymously sped by.

I wonder if it is not the season after the day that is the real gift to us. Maybe it is the reflection we do following Christmas Day that gives meaning and depth to the anxious activity that preceded it. Perhaps that is why the church places three important holidays between Christmas and New Year's: not to exhaust us or overwhelm us, but to remind us of the fullness the season implies. It is as if the church is saying, "Wait! Wait! Don't pack up the Christmas tree, put away the presents, and go shopping for Valentine's Day cards just yet. There is a lot more to Christmas still left. There is important unfinished work we need to face."

The first holy day, December 26, honors St. Stephen. Controversy and bickering had broken out among some of the gentile Christians who claimed they were being discriminated against by Jewish Christians in the distribution of food. Strict adherence to the dietary laws versus a more liberal interpretation for non-Jews was probably the real root of the problem. Stephen and others were appointed to straighten out the mess, smooth ruffled feathers, and encourage an equitable compromise. It was probably a thankless task. Controversy continued to dog Stephen the rest of his life. At one point a mob was incited against him, partly at least because Stephen was also a gifted preacher and then, as is often the case now, ability and innovation in others were resented. Emotions got out of hand and Stephen became the church's first martyr.

December 27 honors John the Apostle and Evangelist. In contrast to Stephen, John was reputed to live to a ripe old age. The apostle John may have had a large part in compiling the Gospel bearing his name, for it is a Gospel told from a different perspective than the others and reveals evidence of eyewitness accounts. John was very concerned that the gospel remain authentic as well as communicate through different cultures. This is one reason his beautiful account of Jesus' birth or origin is so different from Matthew's or Luke's.

The third day, December 28, which completes this cycle, is the remembrance of the Holy Innocents. The prayers for this day are not only for those children killed by Herod in the futile attempt to insure that Jesus would never threaten his throne, but for all innocent victims. At first glance, Herod's action seems unbelievable because it is so horrid. Yet it did happen in some way more than we might think. Nero did the same thing, not to peasant children but to the children of Roman nobility. Nor should we be deluded into thinking it was something done only in a brutal age long past. The killing in Kosovo will not be the last tragedy of this sort either. If in war, truth is said to be the first casualty,[2] in the name of diplomacy and security, children are often the first innocent victims.

Why do we remember all these people and events right after Christmas Day? That is for all of us to think about, not for me to presume to answer for us. I was reminded as I drove on a back highway that the lights of Christmas shine for the Christ child at the stable, they blaze the way to Egypt for the Holy Family, they burn for martyrs such as Stephen and for innocent victims, and they light the darkness in our world, as in John's Gospel. It is a true gift that they shine not for a day, but for a season.

---

2. "The first casualty when war comes is truth," attributed to Senator Hiram Johnson in *The First Casualty: From the Crimea to Vietnam: The War corespondent as hero, propagandist, and myth maker,* by Phillip Knightly (New York; Harcourt, Brace, Jovanovich, 1975), p. v.

Epiphany and Old Snapshots

When they saw that the star had stopped, they were overwhelmed with joy. On entering the house, they saw the child with Mary his mother; and they knelt down and paid him homage. Then, opening their treasure chests, they offered him gifts of gold, frankincense, and myrrh. And having been warned in a dream not to return to Herod, they left for their own country by another road.
Matthew 2:10–12

The three great stories of the Epiphany season are the manifestation of Christ to the gentile world, symbolized by magi from foreign lands guided by a heavenly star to Jesus' birth; the validation of Jesus' ministry by God's Word and the prophets, symbolized by Jesus' baptism by John the Baptist at the Jordan River; and the initial disclosure that Jesus was inaugurating a new kingdom, God's kingdom, symbolized by the great sign at a wedding feast in Cana of Galilee.

Many of you at one time or another have given your children a camera or let them take pictures on a family vacation. You quickly discover that different children like to take pictures of different things, and not necessarily what you would like them to remember. You go to the seashore, and you get back photographs of things that make you wonder if you all went on the same vacation. You load up your child with film and lend your good camera to take on a school field trip to Washington, D.C., and you get back photos of sports cars parked at a rest stop on the New Jersey Turnpike.

The Gospel readings of Epiphany are like different camera shots, taken by different people, that invite us to learn and perceive the great event of God entering the lives of humanity in continually fresh ways. The readings are like the Advent calendars that open new windows, revealing a different scene every day, but always referring to Jesus' birth.

One of the best-loved series of contemporary children's picture books is entitled *Where's Waldo?* by Martin Handford. The books have detailed illustrations of dozens of people, young and old, and all sorts of animals, playing games and working. Somewhere in the picture is this character named Waldo, but you have to look carefully to find him.

John's story of the wedding feast is like a *Where's Waldo?* illustration. It is layer upon layer of symbols that draw us deeper into the meaning of the gospel. The story is not a transcript of how Jesus spoke to his mother, any more than the illustrations of *Where's Waldo?* are photos of an actual scene of dozens of people playing hide-and-go-seek, soccer, and baseball, flying kites, and having picnics all in the same small park at the same time. The story of Jesus' first great sign is about the emptiness of our lives being filled, about the disappointing water the world offers our spirits being changed into a fine refreshment for our souls, about God's generosity and love not being a deception or trick that will be withdrawn as soon as we let down our guard and put our trust in God's grace. The story is about Jesus' knowing beforehand that people will hurt and try to kill him, yet remaining unchanged in his genuine love for all of us. The story is about the hiddenness, the unpretentiousness, and yet the inevitability of the fermentation of God's kingdom to persist and to grow, a sign telling us never to give up hope on ourselves or on others.

At Christmas we invite the children at our parish to come forward and place the sheep around Jesus in the stable. Nativity scenes are hardly historical reconstructions, yet they are a way for youngsters to have a part in our savior's birth. No doubt over the time the nativity scene is on display, it is rearranged several times over by little hands. That's okay, for that helps us to understand that God's love rearranges us, rearranges things in our world, and does not let us go.

As an Epiphany activity, you might get down the old scrapbooks and photos of past vacations. I for one have always wished that the local newspaper every so often would publish a front page of twenty years ago. True, I know how things turned out. But even though we have read it before, even though we were there at the seashore and long ago forgot what we actually did besides driving five hundred miles and eating lukewarm burgers, we might learn and discover that the years open to us another perspective and make God's love in retrospect a little more clearer.

That is why there is wisdom every Epiphany in reading these three strange stories of far-off events, filled with stuff we would not perceive even if we were actually there, of God's rearranging things and of God's offering us an invitation to rearrange our lives.

February Thaw

Jesus took with him Peter, James and his brother John and led them up a high mountain where they could be alone.

Matthew 17:1
The Jerusalem Bible

One Sunday afternoon, the snow in our backyard had melted except for a few hardy patches. Our old Christmas tree lay on its side next to the back of the garage where I had dragged it from the living room one dark night in early January, so I hauled it back into the woods and deposited it into a shallow gully. I looked around and saw that it was joining four or five other trees of Christmas past. Yes, they had all been special trees, good trees, hand picked and cut by two or more Snyders. Our balsam wreath, dried brown by the western sun, was also lying next to the garage and that, too, I placed by the tree.

The calendar of the church year reminds us that transitions are part of the natural order of things. This particular Sunday morning had marked the transition from Epiphany to Lent. The lingering fragrance of Christmas is finally swept away, much as are the last pine needles from under the edge of the rug. For Jesus, the early days of gathering disciples and the exciting freshness of a new initiative are over. The work of discipleship, the preparation for the journey to judgment in Jerusalem begin.

After warning the disciples that they were going to Jerusalem, where things would get nasty and not turn out as the disciples had hoped, Jesus took Peter, James, and John up a high mountain. The air was fresh and clean and the wind seemed to confirm the success of Jesus' mission. I can understand the desire of the three disciples to linger and build structures. I have a friend who once built a fancy tree house for his grandchildren in a huge sycamore in his backyard. He had a high-pressure job dealing with trying to please people, and he was good at it. He'd often remark to me, though, that there were times he'd love to have come home, not tell anyone, and climb up and hide in the tree house. I can sense the disciples' fear of leaving that place and descending from the mountain. It's a natural reluctance and it's okay to name it. They had a strong awareness of the evil spirits of jealousy and ambition that lay ahead, meaner than the spirits of epilepsy or schizophrenia, and they preferred not to face the grueling tests that awaited them.

Standing in the little gully among the former Christmas trees, I relished the quiet. The woods were comfortable and soothing. The birds and squirrels apparently were all taking naps. There were no mosquitoes, and no yelps from my neighbor's swimming pool. I closed my eyes; the sun sure felt good.

"Dad! Dad! Why are you standing so still out there?" a voice broke the spell. "Come inside. You have an important phone call." By summer the trunks and branches of Christmas past will be covered with the brush and vines of new growth. It will probably be a full year before I go back into the woods and stand in that gully again.

Ashes

All are from the dust, and all turn to dust again.
Ecclesiastes 3:20

I first visited New York City with my parents, traveling by car. Later, on my own, I took the bus or train. It was the long tunnels that made the first indelible impression. They all served as a sign of no return with no indication of what was beyond on the other end. One was committed to going forward as the safe, known world was left behind. One now entered the domain of a nether world, where there was no sky, horizon, or point of reference until one came up into the big city itself, looking up at the tall canyon walls of skyscrapers reaching for the heavens.

By and large, transitions are like that: the first day of school, going off to college, job relocation, entering a nursing home, the parting of a loved one at death. We seem to go into a long tunnel before we come out again. Life, even an ordinary life that is not marred by the larger social catastrophes of war, violence, or accidental calamities, means plenty of transitions.

One of the ways we deal with such transitions is to recall happy times of stability in our past. I suspect many a child sent off to a summer camp for the first time thinks of summer visits to grandmother's house, or the smell of Great-Aunt Maude's oatmeal cookies coming out of the oven, as the bus pulls away. High school and college yearbooks are care packages of memories for the journey of transition soon to take place for graduates. Music and poetry of previous decades become geysers of surprising gifts for the aged.

I remember by title only a film called *Nobody Waved Good-bye*. I think it was about someone who decided to leave home and go live someplace else. The implication, of course, and the reason the title haunts me, is that no one cared to notice and to say good-bye. There were no memories of people who said, "We loved you here, we will miss you, and your time with us meant something."

Church holidays tie together our personal life with the experiences of many others. When we are unable to affirm our relationship with God, a larger community helps to do it for us. Ash Wednesday, the beginning of Lent, is a transition from the levity of winter carnivals to a more somber hungering for spring. Yes, there will still be a few good skiing trips left, but the seed, flower, and camping catalogues that begin to arrive in the mail are welcomed.

Ashes used to be part of our everyday experience when we burned coal and wood in our stoves and furnaces. For those of us without wood stoves, ashes are a quaint reminder of the past, like the tin shovels, ash buckets, and ice picks hanging in every antique shop. Ashes, however, remain a symbol reminding us all too well that we are transitory material like everything on this earth. Part of maturity is coming to terms with the fact that nothing on this earth is permanent and forever. Dust to dust—even as we shake the dust off our feet hurrying on the way to somewhere else.

Yet we are very special dust to God. We are noticed, we are missed, and we are longed after. Ash Wednesday also announces the Good News that God is in our past, among us in the present, and will be there in our future. I suspect the so-called Book of Judgment isn't a ledger of accounts at all; it's more like a school yearbook, full of silly and informal snapshots, taken over time and often when we were not looking. Through our many transitions, I wonder if God doesn't enjoy turning the pages, adding pictures and pasting them in, chuckling at the funny ones, weeping at the poignant ones, and pondering where our journey will take us next.

Holy Week: The Bonds of Our Common Humanity

After a little while the bystanders came up and said to Peter, "Certainly you are also one of them, for your accent betrays you." Then he began to curse, and he swore an oath, "I do not know the man!" At that moment the cock crowed. Then Peter remembered what Jesus had said: "Before the cock crows, you will deny me three times." And he went out and wept bitterly.

Matthew 26:73–75

It's been years ago, but my memory of her still makes me uneasy. During my first months at a new parish I discovered that the local synagogue had a wonderful tradition of holding an open house on a Sunday, after the services of the downtown churches. There were tours, discussion groups, and best of all, a bountiful kosher luncheon. All the synagogue requested was a reservation beforehand. On the Sunday of the reception, I knew a number of us planned to attend, but right before the later service, a certain woman came up and announced to me that she was going too. She had been attending our church for several months, and when she took her medication properly, she was able to handle herself pretty well. Yet it was obvious that she had been struggling with the demons of mental illness for years and occasionally she had a sharp tongue that got out of control. "Uh, oh,"

I thought to myself. Something told me it wasn't a good idea, but I replied, "Okay, why don't you wait for me after the service, and then we will walk over together."

After the service, I waited at the front steps, but she was nowhere to be found. Whew, I thought with relief, I missed the bullet this time. Down the street I went. When I arrived at the synagogue I was warmly greeted and introduced. Soon, however, I heard her voice above the noise of the reception. Unfortunately she was saying some very inappropriate remarks, always ending with "and I am with him," pointing over to me. She was across the room, and it was impossible to catch her eye. Even if I had, I suspect any attempt to turn the conversation would only have made things worse. What I could do was blush, and I'm told that is one thing I do quite well on occasion. One of the older leaders of the synagogue quickly understood the situation and perceived my discomfort. Without hesitation he put his firm arm around my shoulders, and with a knowing and comforting smile, reassured me; "Don't worry. We know our rabbi has to deal with some very difficult congregants, too."

What a gift of hospitality! But the greater gift was yet to come. I issued a profound "thank you," I was about to add, "But she isn't really one of us; she doesn't belong to my parish. I barely know her. She just wandered in off the streets and came through the door," when I realized, How dare I! Of course she is part of us;

she is one of us; I do know her, and that can never be denied. It was then that I understood that I had been given an even more important, if salient, gift.

I have not seen her for years. After a few more weeks, she stopped coming to church, although she would occasionally phone me at home. I am afraid that she had to be institutionalized permanently and that she is still struggling with powerful demons. She may well be a shriveled old woman now, never visited, and avoided when possible by the staff. Yet she is still one of us, and I continue to remember her. Especially during the last weeks of Lent and Holy Week, a phrase from the marriage service frequently comes into my mind: "that the bonds of our common humanity, by which all your children are united one to another, and the living to the dead, may be so transformed by your grace." *Remember the common bonds of our humanity* is what Holy Week whispers. Jesus never denies or breaks the bond. Even from the cross, the common bond of our humanity is affirmed. God never wavers.

Opening Day

Philip said to him, "Lord show us the Father and we will be satisfied." Jesus said to him, "Have I been with you all this time, Philip, and you still do not know me?..."

John 14:8–9

In New York state, Easter season usually coincides with the opening of trout season. Inevitably I am fortunate to be invited on a trip with fishermen who are much more skilled and serious than I. My companions come with several antique fly rods, dozens of hand-tied flies, and volumes of information about hatches. "Hmm,'" they say as they open one of their fly boxes. "I'd like to use a montreal or black gnat, but look at that hatch over the water. Maybe a brown hackle would be better. What do you think, Philip? This stretch of water calls for a streamer, don't you think?" "Hmm," I reply. "Yes, indeed." I let them finally suggest what fly to use. After I go through my vest pockets, mumbling words like muddler minnow, gray ghost, and warden's worry, they proudly give me one of theirs. The truth is, of course, I have only three or four flies: a red one, a silver one, and one with a funny big yellow feather.

"Lord, you don't need to show me a miracle, just show me a fish," I pray. I've dreamt of somehow hooking and landing a trophy specimen that all my companions will admire. My picture will be taken for posterity. "What did you use?" "Oh, I used a special streamer, a white buck tail, fished as a nymph. Works every time." But it's never happened. If I catch a small chub this early in the season, I'm lucky.

In that compressed period between Jesus' resurrection and the ascension, I wonder if Jesus was not trying to teach Thomas and Philip something about the real nature of ministry. I can picture Philip and Thomas wanting Jesus to take them fishing. "Show us a place where the trophy fish are," they plead. So Jesus smiles and takes them down to a stream. There they get the shock of their lives, for Jesus tells them, "I am not interested in a trophy for you to display on your wall and something for you to brag about. I'm here to show you how to fish for food, how to feed and nourish your family." With that, Jesus pulls out a cheap fiberglass casting rod. The disciples are aghast. But it gets worse, much worse. Jesus then reaches into a brown paper bag and pulls out a white plastic container of worms. Jesus uses bait! (Jesus knows, especially in spring, it is fat, wiggly worms, not carefully matched flies, that the fish love to take.)

I've been fortunate to be part of church communities large and small in which people lovingly ministered to each other. The backbone of such work is a quiet, unpretentious effort that rarely leads to the formation of ingenious programs that would attract the attention of the larger church. The fruit of its ministry hasn't produced an incredible drawing card, bringing in hoards of new people or bags of gold. It is unlikely to win any recognition from a bishop or district superintendent. Yet, in such caring we have fed and sustained one other. We have talked, listened, shared, and cried together. We have not tried to impress each other or change each other with our superior knowledge of flies and hatches. Instead of fishing for trophies to hang in our club room, we have sought food for each other. Like Jesus, we have been simple, lowly bait fishermen. We've left all the fancy equipment we've collected and the accouterments of the esoteric expertise we are so proud of behind in the car.

Traveling the Road to Emmaus

Jesus himself came up and walked by their side; but something prevented them from recognizing him.

Luke 24:15, The Jerusalem Bible

In college, I spent many happy summers as a camp counselor in Maine and hated to leave at the end of August. For a few of the staff, there was an informal reunion around the last week of September, at the Fryeburg Fair, a regional agricultural fair complete with demolition derby and carnival midway. I was never able to go, for I lived too far away until I entered seminary in Massachusetts. So, with one week of seminary behind me, I left for a wonderful weekend in Maine, and even won a large stuffed animal at the ring toss.

The day after I returned was the reception given by the dean and his wife for all incoming students. I was happily eating the stuffed mushrooms when the dean's wife came over to introduce herself. "Oh," she smiled when she found out I had gone to Maine over the weekend. "Did you enjoy the leaves?"

My mind went blank. Demolition derbies, sideshows, games, the smell of vinegar and French fries, nothing seemed to come forth that was associated with leaves. "Leaves?" I repeated.

"Yes, leaves," the dean's wife emphatically repeated. "How were the leaves?" I noticed the plate of mushrooms on the leaf of the table and knew I needed to make a good impression. However, it was noisy in the room, perhaps I had misunderstood.

"Leaves?" I kept saying. At this point the dean's wife had obviously come to a rather unflattering conclusion about a certain member of the incoming class.

"Yes, leaves, leaves, you know the things that grow on trees." Well, hey, I was on board now, and quickly replied, "Oh, you mean leaves!" At that point the dean's wife had gained all she wanted to know about me.

Later in the evening I thought I saw her nudge her husband and imagined her saying, "You see that dull fellow over there by the empty mushroom platter? He is never going to make it through your Old Testament class."

The two disciples on the road to Emmaus had a lot on their minds. They were not in the absolute depths of despair, but they didn't know how to process the signs of hope that three of their number had given them. They needed a weekend away, to clear their heads, to get some fresh air. As they walked and talked, a stranger joined them. He seemed to be a sympathetic listener and was invited to be part of the conversation. He was obviously well trained in the Scriptures and was a great help in pointing out insights they had not even thought of. They invited him to stay for dinner and spend the night.

Although he was someone they had just met, he seemed like an old familiar teacher, and as evening wore on, the role of host and guest seemed to become blurred. They talked and asked questions far into the night. The story, as we have it, suggests that when they recognized him as the risen Lord, he left. Perhaps the disciples wanted to emphasize that while Jesus will come among us, we cannot hold or control him. Perhaps they had talked until they all fell asleep and in the wee hours of the night they awoke with a start and knew Jesus had been there.

How much the evening reminded them of the Last Supper when Jesus talked about a new way of living with one another and a new kind of relationship with God. How much this stranger who had walked with them reminded them of the way of their rabbi. The words and actions of Jesus came back to them and as they remembered, they began to understand that the Last Supper with Jesus a few days ago was also the first meal of resurrection until the end of time.

We treat the things we associate with Communion as holy things, and rightly so. Yet, there is also a danger of making Jesus into some sort of magician, as if by sleight of hand we find something has been changed. Jesus is not trying to deceive or fool us. The Last Supper is not a magic show. Rather it has helped people of faith reflect, remember, and ponder what has been present all the time. Jesus didn't hide himself from or try to deceive those on the Emmaus road. They were simply unable to see him other than as a stranger. What we can surmise from our own experience is that, in God's time and way, an incomprehensible puzzle gradually began to make sense.

The dean's wife wasn't trying to trick me. She genuinely wanted to get to know me and asked a perfectly straightforward question when the New England foliage was at its glorious height. But my mind was elsewhere, and I was too full of stuffed mushrooms.

The road to Emmaus does tend to wind through the experiences of volunteering for a task or helping someone out and discovering that we received far more than we gave. The journey does offer great blessings, some of which come after a good night's sleep. On the road to Emmaus, there are inevitably those low times when what we think of as the end of the line later becomes the starting point of another beginning. We are all still on the road to Emmaus, and the Last Supper of Jesus is still a foretaste and benchmark for the discoveries ahead. Just one last word of advice: if you are ever invited into the habitations of deans and presidents, go easy on the stuffed mushrooms.

Snappy's Service

Eight days later the disciples were in the house again and Thomas was with them. The doors were closed, but Jesus came in and stood among them. "Peace be with you," he said.

John 20:26, The Jerusalem Bible

Before the age of flavored coffees, Starbuck's coffee chains, and organic yuppie drinks, each region of the country seemed to have its own distinctive brew. Maine was known for coffee that grew hair on boulders. In the Mid-Atlantic states it wasn't quite as thick, but it was consistently robust. Places that skimped on fresh grounds were shunned as purveyors of "church coffee," suitable only for unsuspecting transients. In the Midwest, people drank more coffee, but considerably weaker than in the Northeast. I reckon three cups of Midwest coffee would make one decent cup of New York coffee.

So it was quite an adjustment when I moved to Iowa from the Adirondacks. A major task was finding a place that had coffee that had more body than dishwater. It wasn't easy, but I finally found the place. Most people would have passed it by, and I don't know what ever possessed me to try it in the first place. I must have been really desperate for a taste of home. I learned later that my poor secretary could always tell I had been there by the sheen of my hair and the smell of my sport coat. Thankfully, I was aired out before I did afternoon calling.

Most of the buildings around it were vacant and peeling. It was downtown in a drab section, by a bridge over the railroad tracks, a small low appendage to a brick warehouse, a coffee and lunch spot called Snappy's Service. There were no more than six stools at the counter, and when you sat down there you could feel the heat from the fryer. There were three or four small tables, but they were always taken. Actually, you had to time your visit or you would never get a stool. I was honored that somehow as a newcomer, room was made and I was allowed a stool between 10:15 and 11. A ham hock was always near the griddle for those who wanted ham with their eggs. The luncheon menu was mashed potatoes, meat loaf, and gravy. I think Snappy sensed that I had a weak spot for his fried donuts and strong coffee, and this was the only place for miles one could get that combination. I was tolerated there, no questions asked, although Snappy knew I didn't really belong among the bus drivers and city laborers.

A cup and a half of coffee with one donut two or three times a week was all my intestines (and parish secretary) could tolerate, but there came a day, when I was facing some well-publicized challenges, that I had to escape and went down, well past my allotted time on the stool. As I entered through the small door, a stool was suddenly available. Snappy looked up and sympathetically smiled as he said, "Reverend, you need a cup of coffee." Those around me seemed to grunt and ahem in agreement. I knew I was not only tolerated, but accepted. They all understood why I was there.

Some people find Jesus in a great blaze of light that brings them to their knees. Others, like the apostle Thomas, discover that Jesus enters much more quietly. Even though it was dark and the doors were shut, Jesus slipped in and found a place. We do not know if Thomas ever actually put out his hands and felt Jesus' scars. What we *do* know is that *Jesus* touched Thomas. Faith is never a matter of seeing or knowing all the answers, as much as it is a matter of knowing that in some indelible way God's grace has touched us.

For some reason, whenever I read about Thomas during the Easter season, I think of that hole in the wall, way back in Iowa. It was probably condemned and torn down years ago, and now is just a parking lot for an urban center that was never built. I'm one of those who never met Jesus in a sudden blaze of light. Yet I remember that day at Snappy's Service when a big guy in a tee shirt and apron pushed a mug of coffee across the counter and grinned. "Reverend, you need a cup of coffee." Not exactly the same, I suppose, as the "Peace of the Lord be always with you," but then that part of the Midwest was never much on fancy ceremony or sophistication. Yet, I can tell you that in that insignificant hole in the wall, I recall vividly God's peace was passed to me, and I think I know what Thomas was talking about as he witnessed to the living God.

The Current River: We're All Together Again

There is a river, whose streams refresh the city of God.
                                                    Psalm 46:4, The Jerusalem Bible

It started when a group of former Boy Scout leaders got together and reminisced. "Remember how much fun we had taking the boys down the Current River?" said one. "Yes," said another, "and think how much fun we could have if we went down again with just ourselves." So it began, an annual trip of three or four days, down two of the most scenic rivers of America. The Current and its little brother, the Jack's Fork, are spring fed and fast running. Yet they are fairly easy rivers to navigate, with few real rapids. They cut their way through cliffs, jagged rock formations, and forests, fed by frigid bubbling springs and passing cool caves. Natural chutes are formed around their sand banks and will take you for a brisk ride, inviting you to splash back and let the river zip you down the chute all over again.

One year I was fortunate enough to be invited to join this merry group of about a dozen. After breakfast an old school bus, pulling a trailer loaded with canoes, arrived at our cabins to take us to the put-in place. As we bumped down the road, we sang the old camp song, *We're all together again, we're here, we're here.*

...ether again, we're here, we're here. Who knows when we'll be all together ...ere, we're here. Tradition was satisfied.

...ere bakers, businessmen, teachers, lawyers, entrepreneurs, ministers, you ...e it. We all had lived different lives. Yet on the river, we discovered that we ...idn't have to be rich to have fun. We could leave behind all the status larger society claims we need to make our way and still make our journey, enjoying the adventure and savoring each other's company. By common consent we declared that "what happens on the river, stays on the river." Actually, there was nothing profound or scandalous to write about anyway, and that's worth noting. Some of us enjoyed watching the hawks catching the updrafts off the cliffs or the fish in the clear water. We stopped when we felt like it. We had no schedule or deadline. We didn't need to paddle and as long as we stayed in the canoes and avoided the root wads, the current of the river itself would take us down to our take-out place in plenty of time.

There was one important rule imposed on us. You didn't fight the current. It was too powerful. You let it carry you, and if it bumped you around, it was dangerous to strike back. If somehow your canoe got caught broadside it was far better to be prepared to let the flow dump you into the water and let it bump you around the log or rock.

It was very much unlike how most of us have to behave in the world. W are expected to strive and fight back. In the church, for example, we have lost much of the status within larger society we had in the 1950s. It is more of a challenge finding Sunday school teachers, members of property committees, and bazaar chairs. Some blame the lack of competent and creative leadership, or the increased pressures of work, or the banality of the tasks. But the main reason, I suspect, is much more sobering: society itself was our main recruiting agent, but no longer is willing to play that role, and we have not found a replacement. In other words we are being confronted with a destiny vis-à-vis larger society that is not in our hands. The current of society is running its own course and we don't have control. We may deny it or angrily try to fight to regain it, and we simply can't.

One of the greatest miscalculations we can make is to assume that discipleship today is easy. Discipleship has a cost, and society offers some pretty strong and compelling alternatives to follow. Don't underestimate society's currents and undertows.

On the river, we knew we didn't have total control. We recognized our limits and unclenched our fists. We stayed clear of root wads and didn't try to gun the canoes through them. We had respect for the currents. We let the river take us; we

d enjoyed the float. Late afternoon, we arrived at the take-out place,
nd tired. Our bodies told us we weren't young campers any longer.
dreaming of sleeping out underneath the stars, we yearned for hot
rs and shampoo for our hair. The old bus pulled up to meet us. As we
mbed on and slid into the green neoprene seats, I knew that I had been given
a great gift. We had survived all the world had thrown at us, and we could still
laugh and have just as much fun as when we were naive, innocent kids. The first
song of morning came back to me. *We're all together again, we're here, we're here.*
We're all together again, we're here, we're here. Who knows when we'll be all together
again, we're here, we're here.

The Last Walk of Autumn

Later on, Jesus showed himself again to the disciples. It was by the Sea of Tiberias, and it happened like this. Simon Peter, Thomas called the twin, Nathanael from Cana in Galilee, the sons of Zebedee and two more of his disciples were together. Simon Peter said, "I'm going fishing." They replied, "We'll come with you." They went out and got into the boat but caught nothing that night. It was light by now and there stood Jesus on the shore, though the disciples did not realize that it was Jesus. Jesus called out, "Have you caught anything, friends?" And when they answered "No," he said, "Throw the net out to starboard and you'll find something." So they dropped the net, and there were so many fish that they could not haul it in. The disciple Jesus loved said to Peter, "It is the Lord."

John 21:1–6, The Jerusalem Bible

S ome years ago, I went with two fishing buddies on a fall fishing expedition at the end of the season. The Adirondack foliage was at its peak on one of those perfect days that start out with a crisp breeze nudging the trees and later warm up to the mid-seventies. I had mixed feelings, knowing it would be one of the last trips I would take with these particular friends, for I had accepted a new position and was moving to a different part of the country in January. We hiked down the

g banks of moss and ground pine still lush and green, with red and
_ leaves falling upon us. In a way, death was all around us, but it was
_ was so beautiful that it was hard to be afraid. I sensed a voice telling
_at it was a natural transition, both for the woods and for me. I somehow
_ealized that such memories of this trip would give me the strength to live through
the deaths and transitions that were ahead. In the long winter when I would miss
my friends and the familiar mountains and never see anything but bleak fields, I
would remember.

I did not get up that morning expecting to find God or to learn some profound lesson of life. Yet I sensed a close presence in those woods telling me that
I would be given the fortitude to live through the deaths and transitions to come
and that memories of beauty are legitimate handholds to grab tightly. Several
years later, my fishing buddies and I did get together again to reminisce about old
times. We recalled that fall day and how special it was for all of us. (None of us
remembered if we caught any fish.)

With effort, I could find the steam again and with luck even the thick banks
of moss. But certainly it would not be the same. I'm not sure we can ever re-
create moments of grace. Moreover, had I gone that morning intending to find a
moment that would have held vivid significance to me, I question whether I
would have discovered or remembered anything at all. Revelations don't occur on

a demand basis. That is why crusades to find the Holy usually fail and techniques to guarantee profound encounters are ephemeral at best. And it is why when people yearn for a spiritual experience, I'm inclined to say don't push it or try too hard. Be good to yourself. Make some homemade ice cream, reserve some time to play with children, or take the dog for a walk. Take the last walk of autumn. Like other less-desirable attributes of existence, grace happens. It simply happens: it's a gift, and that's good news.